DATING

DATING

Surviving and thriving in the social scene

BRENTON G. YORGASON

Bookcraft
Salt Lake City, Utah

Library of Congress Catalog Card Number: 95-80175
ISBN 1-57008-183-2

First Printing, 1995

Printed in the United States of America

This book is dedicated to the young people who have welcomed me into their lives, and their hearts, to discuss the most exciting yet often complex world of dating and relating.

Contents

Introduction

Two decades ago, while teaching seminary at Maryvale High School in Phoenix, Arizona, I became reacquainted and fascinated with the totally awesome world of dating. Not that I hadn't enjoyed the pleasures and perils of dating a decade earlier than that, when I had been deeply entrenched in the dating scene, because I certainly had. But now, as a seasoned married man of six years and a father of three preschool-age sons, I could look into the world of my students through an entirely different and clearly detached lens. You see, I had matured well beyond my twenty-eight years, and had gained perspective which I could share.

A year later, after being transferred to the East High seminary in Salt Lake City, Utah, my eyes were opened even more to the increasingly sophisticated art form of dating. I could hardly believe how much more creative and complex the dating exploits of my students had become . . . and I thought *I* was a source of learning for *them*. Actually, I suppose that I have learned much more from watching students and my own teenagers date and interact with members of the opposite sex than I ever have from a class or a book!

It was while teaching seminary at East, and then later at Skyline High School, that I began to pen my growing impressions about dating. At last, and much to my surprise (and I think the surprise of everyone who knew me), I completed the manuscript of my first book, *From First Date to Chosen Mate*. That was nearly twenty years ago, and yet the laughs and tears I have shared with my young friends as they read these pages are as fresh and real today as they were then.

And so today, with an even deeper love for young people, I again take pen in hand. This time, however I do so with the aid of my trusty computer. My intent is to share ideas that are both old and new. In this regard, I have incorporated into the present volume material from that first book on dating, though in many cases I have done a good deal of reworking and updating.

It is my hope that you, as a teenager or young adult, will enjoy the pages that follow. This may even be the first book you will have chosen to read and study outside of school, and may open a whole new world of enjoyment to you. It may also be just one book in a large stack that you have ventured into recently. Whatever the case, perhaps a few thoughts in this book will take root in your heart and assist you in successfully passing through the remaining "single" years of your life, as you prepare yourself for an eternal temple marriage. If so, then the time and energy spent in putting them in book form will have been well worth it. Whether you are fifteen and looking forward to your first date or you are twenty-four and still single, the pages that follow are for you.

Now, close the door to your room, put in your newest CD, curl up with your favorite blanket, and enjoy!

POP
CORN

1

First Date

The first date with someone can tend to be an unsettling experience. What is really going on in the mind of the other person? In this chapter I adapt the words of an author I have been unable to identify, as he represents the feelings and mutual misinterpretations possible on such a date.

As Seen Through the Eyes of Tausha

I was anxiously putting on my lipstick for the fifth time when the doorbell rang. As I heard its familiar chime, about eight thousand butterflies took wing in my stomach. Believe it or not, I had waited an entire year for this night. I had thought Josh was never going to take the hint and ask me out. Now, as my hand shook uncontrollably, I knew that if this evening didn't turn out to be perfect, he'd never ask me out again.

With that discomforting thought in mind, I tried to quiet my knocking knees. I then took a deep breath, walked down the hallway, and opened the door.

Josh stood on the front doorstep, the porch light blazing down on the gorgeous smooth hair every girl in school would love to run her fingers through. It was fact—Josh Jenkins was the pure dripping hunk of the last days!

"Hi," he whispered, smiling cheerfully, "you look nice."

I didn't look nice at all. My hair hadn't turned out, and my favorite dress had been inadvertently left at the cleaners.

I smiled back anyway, feeling it was more of a wince than a genuine smile. "Thanks, so do you," I answered, and immediately wished I hadn't. How totally dumb can you get? You just don't say that kind of thing to a guy—even when his "totally rad" appearance melts your heart all the way down to your stomach.

A moment later, when we were settled in his nearly new Geo Prizm, Josh turned to me and asked, "Where would you like to go?"

When he asked the question, something in the area of my midsection dropped ten feet. That wasn't fair! How did I know where he could afford to go? And how totally dull he's going to think I am if I don't suggest something exciting. My father had warned that this should have been a double date, and now I was beginning to believe him. Josh had successfully placed the entire burden of the evening on *my* shoulders, and there was simply nothing I could do about it.

"Wherever you want to go," I finally said, chalking up the second point against me. I was in rare form tonight. I'd managed to be both dumb and dull in less than two minutes. And, I had a feeling this was only the beginning.

Josh looked and smiled again—or pretended to, anyway.

"How about going to the Villa?"

Then something dropped ten more feet. The Villa was an ancient movie theater nearby, on Highland Drive.

"I've seen the movie," I said miserably. Tausha Blackwell, girl failure.

Josh thought for a moment. "How about the Starlight?"

I coughed violently. The Starlight was a drive-in theater. No drive-ins for me. That was kind of a rule my friends and I had. "I've seen that movie, too," I lied, wondering what was playing and praying he wouldn't ask. I also wished I were dead.

Josh looked as if he was going to laugh, but he didn't.

"What movie *haven't* you seen?" he asked, almost in a whisper.

"Spielberg's PG-13 one at the Southtown Mall," I said weakly. I'd seen that one too, but at this moment I wouldn't have admitted it under oath.

This time Josh did laugh, right out loud. In fact, he laughed several times on the way to the mall, and I chalked up several more points against me.

Nothing disastrous happened between the parking lot and the lobby, and I was beginning to relax when he walked over to the refreshment stand. He then gave me a questioning look. Assuming that he was asking if I wanted something, I shook my head no.

Then, without speaking, he ordered two boxes of popcorn—with extra butter—and promptly handed me one. He'd mistaken my nod to mean yes, and somehow that figured. What difference did it make that I despised popcorn, not to mention *buttered* popcorn? It gave me the world's noisiest hiccups every time I even looked at it! Nothing had gone right so far, so why should it start now?

Spielberg's movie—which, by the way, I hadn't seen once; I'd seen it twice—was about one-fourth over when I realized Josh wasn't watching the movie. He was watching me! That figured, too. There I was, gazing vacantly at the screen, clutching the still-full box of popcorn like it was an old friend.

"Don't you want your popcorn?" he asked when our eyes met.

"Of course," I blurted, much too loudly.

Someone behind us said, "Shut up!" in a very impolite tone of voice.

Returning my vacant gaze to the screen, I bravely ventured my hand into the greasy box of popcorn. I ate one kernel, and held my breath. Nothing happened. I ate another kernel, and then I hiccuped so resoundingly that it was heard all over the theater. Although I'd been expecting it to happen, the hiccup startled me so much that the entire box of popcorn spilled all over Josh's lap. Then I started to laugh. I tried not to, but I just couldn't help myself. Then that aforementioned someone behind us told us to shut up this time or else. I did.

Solemnly but silently swearing never to open my ridiculous mouth again as long as I lived, I watched the remainder of the movie without seeing it. All through it I was conscious, too conscious, of Josh beside me. How I loved the thought of his being there, and the knowledge that he'd never be there again made me want to start bawling. Considering my track record for the evening, it's a wonder I didn't go right ahead and bawl.

After the movie, we went to the Iceberg. This was a local fast-food drive-in that had been fashioned after the carhop drive-ins of the 1950s and '60s. It was then that I began to wonder what I'd ever done to deserve all this.

Josh ordered a famous chocolate shake, and a hamburger *with* onions!

The waitress looked at me; I looked back at the waitress; she looked back at me. "Well?" she said at last, and not too kindly.

Well what? If I didn't order a hamburger, Josh was going to think I didn't want to kiss him good night. I wasn't going to kiss him anyway—another of those rules. But I didn't want to give him the idea I wanted him to kiss me—which I did, but wouldn't—if you know what I mean.

I sighed wholeheartedly. "I'll have a cup of water, and a . . . a burger *without*." And I'll be darned if Josh didn't laugh again. My face flamed, and when our order arrived, I bit into my burger like I expected it to bite me back.

When the waitress came back to pick up the tray, Josh looked at his watch. "Hey, it's after eleven!" he said, sounding worried. "I've got to get home. I've got basketball in the morning."

I made myself nod politely. Basketball practice, my eye! On Saturday? Precisely who was he trying to kid? Me, that's who. I even knew what would come next. We'd drive home and he would walk me to the door. He'd say it had been fun and that he'd call me. And he never would. That was perfectly all right with me because I wouldn't come to the phone, anyway. Future conversations were out of the question!

We drove home, and Josh walked me to the door. "It's been fun," he said. "I'll call you," he added.

Then, instead of trying to kiss me good night, or asking if he could, Josh simply reached up and patted me on the head. Patted me! I fully expected him to say, "Good night, Rover," but he didn't. He just said good night and sprinted back to the Geo.

When I got up to my room, I thought about Josh and our date. What a total disaster!

I wound my hair spitefully on my mother's outdated rollers, then went to bed feeling that I wouldn't be able to sleep a wink.

I fell asleep immediately, hoping morning would never come.

As Seen Through the Eyes of Josh

I must have stood on Tausha's doorstep for at least five full minutes before I rang the bell. For some crazy reason, I suddenly didn't want to go out with Tausha. It wasn't because she wasn't cute or popular; she was that and a lot more. I guess it was because I knew it was going to be like all the other dates I went on.

You see, although I don't really know why, the girls around school consider me some kind of a catch or something. As far as I can see, about the only thing that makes me any different from the rest of the guys is that I'm available. I've never gone steady in my life! And you know what that does to a girl. What I *have* done is play football—tight end, actually. I've also belonged to A Cappella, Madrigals, Singers Unlimited, and of course the National Honor Society. Advanced Placement classes have also become routine, and I guess with all of these extra-effort involvements, the girls are quick to notice.

I didn't have to wonder if Tausha was going to act just like the other girls who had tried to snare me. I knew. She had sort of a thing for me, and had had it for a long time. Now that I had asked her out for a date, I knew what was in store for me.

For the next four hours, Tausha was going to do everything she could to make sure her hooks got into me but solid. She was going to be perfect. She'd look perfect, act perfect, and try everything in her power to give me the "ten feet tall" feeling that some girls have the mistaken idea they're capable of giving.

Tonight she'd be an alluring, willing slave to the poor defenseless male she hoped to master. Unfortunately, that poor defenseless male was me.

But, what the heck. I rang the doorbell anyway.

I must say that when Tausha answered the door, I immediately knew I'd been right about one thing. She did look perfect.

I smiled. "Hi," I said, "you look nice."

She smiled back. "Thanks, so do you."

So do you? That was a weird thing for a girl to say. They usually expect a guy to spend about two years getting all shaved and dressed up for them, but he's the one who has to dish out the compliments.

A moment later, when we settled in my father's Geo, I had every intention of starting and heading for Southtown Mall. It was playing the only movie I hadn't seen; but I just couldn't resist asking a question I already knew the answer to.

Turning to her, I said, "Where would you like to go?"

She, of course, would have a list of exciting places to mention, just so I'd think she was about the coolest girl alive.

"Wherever you want to go," she replied.

That was a surprise! But I knew she'd rise to the bait on the next question.

"How about going to the Villa?" I knew she'd seen that movie because I'd seen her there two nights before. But she'd never admit to it on a bet. It wouldn't be the perfect thing to do.

"I've seen the movie," Tausha said at last.

Okay, I thought, *have it your way. Don't try to be perfect. Try to be different. That's a good form of attraction, too.* Now, what would a girl who is trying to be different do to prove it?

"How about the Starlight?" I asked, which was a stroke of sheer genius. Most of the girls had some silly rule about no drive-ins on dates, but not when they're trying to be different.

Tausha caught her breath and coughed as if she had just swallowed the answer to my question. "I've seen that movie, too," she lied hopefully. I don't know why I knew she was lying—I just did—and all of a sudden I felt like laughing.

"What movie *haven't* you seen?" I asked, knowing she wouldn't name one playing at the mall, because that's where I wanted to go—the only non-R-rated movie I hadn't seen was playing there.

She looked very perplexed for a second (this kid must go to an awful lot of movies), and then she spoke. "Spielberg's PG-13 one at the Southtown Mall."

I don't know why that made me feel like laughing again, but this time I couldn't keep from doing it. It must have been that odd look on her face or something. And every time I thought about it on the way to Southtown, I laughed some more. She didn't say anything. She just sort of looked like she was counting something in her head. Probably totaling up the number of movies she'd been to this week.

When we reached the lobby, I asked her if she wanted something, and she waved her head around a couple of times. Rather than go through the trouble of figuring out whether she meant yes or no, I bought her a box of popcorn and let it go at that.

The movie was about one-fourth of the way through when I had the sudden urge to look over at her. She was staring at the screen with that glassy-eyed look people get when they're watching a television rerun for the three-thousandth time. And she was clutching her medium-size container of popcorn like it was an old friend.

I figured the glassy-eyed look out right away. The little devil had seen the movie before; but then, at the rate she went to the movies, how could she have helped it? But the popcorn-clutching bit—that I didn't get.

"Don't you want your popcorn?" I asked, figuring I'd eat it if she didn't.

"Of course," she blurted, in the loudest whisper I think I've ever heard, and stuck her hand in the popcorn box as though she thought it had spiders or something in it. Then she started eating popcorn, holding her breath, then eating more popcorn and holding her breath some more. I was about to ask her what in the something-or-other she was up to when she practically rocked the theater with the biggest, loudest hiccup in history! And that's not all. It frightened her so much that she jumped and the entire box of popcorn landed all over my lap.

Instead of running out of the theater or crawling under her seat from embarrassment, she did the craziest thing. She burst out laughing! I wanted to join her, but some guy behind us started complaining. After that hiccup, he sort of had a point, too.

I have to admit that I watched the rest of the movie without really seeing it. Boy, if this wasn't the weirdest date I'd ever been on in my life.

On the way home from the movie, I dared to make a last attempt. This girl had to do something normal. The law of averages proved that. So I drove into the Iceberg and dropped the bomb.

In addition to one of their famous shakes, I ordered a hamburger *with*. The minute I did it I felt sorry. That's just about the dirtiest trick a guy can pull on a first date. It completely wipes the girl out. She doesn't know what to do. If she orders the same, she thinks the boy thinks she wants him to kiss her good night, which she does, but she won't let him if he tries. On the other hand, if she orders a hamburger *without* onions, she thinks the boy is going to think she doesn't want to kiss him—and she doesn't want that to happen, either. I often wonder about girls, don't you?

Every time I've pulled this on a girl, she's risen above the entire matter and solved everything by ordering a root beer. I waited for Tausha to do just that.

It's a good thing I didn't hold my breath waiting, because after the waitress prompted Tausha a little, she said, "I'll have a cup of water, and a . . . a burger *without*." The way she emphasized *without* just about cracked me up. She got all red, and all of a sudden I felt totally sorry for her.

Then I remembered about tomorrow. I had a basketball practice at 9:00 A.M. My coach really had a heart, but I suppose with such a big game coming up, he wasn't taking any chances.

"Hey," I said, looking at my watch, "it's after eleven. I've got to get home. I've got basketball in the morning."

Tausha's reaction really took the cake.

You know how girls get when they think you've given them the business. They give you this big "I couldn't care less" look, and act like they can hardly wait to get rid of you.

Tausha made an attempt to wave her head around, but her eyes looked like a couple of stones. She not only felt unhappy, but she was totally angry! She plain didn't believe me, and it showed. It was about the most honest reaction I've ever seen a girl have.

I wanted to say something else, but since I couldn't think of anything, I kept quiet until we got to her house. At the door, I knew what I wanted to say, yet I couldn't say it. Something really crummy was happening to me. I was flipping over this girl. She was so cute and so screwy, and her hooks were getting into me but good!

"It's been fun," I said after we had stood on the doorstep looking at each other for what seemed like a week. That was a pretty stupid thing to say, I know, but what was I supposed to say, "I love you"? If I did that, she would probably get the hiccups again and wake up the whole neighborhood. Besides, I didn't. Or did I? Oh well, who knows about stuff like that, anyway?

She didn't say anything at all, but she smiled at me sort of strangely. "I'll call you," I continued. I wanted to kiss her so much I could taste it. But I could also taste those darn onions, so I decided against it.

Instead, I reached up and touched her hair. It came out more like a pat on the head, but it was better than nothing.

With that, I knew I'd better get out of here or I would be coming on strong, onions and all. I practically sprinted back to the car.

All the way home I wondered when to call her. I felt like calling her that night, but no girl is going to wind me around her little finger! I'd wait and call her in the morning before I went to basketball practice. Sure, it'd be pretty early, but she was one girl who didn't need her beauty sleep. And how!

When I arrived home, I chewed a couple of pieces of gum so I could stand to be in the same room with myself and those stupid onions. Then I crawled into bed, knowing I was too keyed up to sleep a wink. Imagine me, ol' Josh Jenkins, trapped! Just the thought of it was enough to scare a guy awake for the next eleven years.

I fell asleep immediately, wishing morning would hurry up.

2

Be Not Half, but Whole

When counseling young people who have announced that they are "in love"—regardless of whether they are in their teens or older—I have often shared with them the notion that two half-persons don't create a whole marriage. To the contrary, it takes two "whole" people to make a relationship work—and you can't begin to mend a low self-concept the week you become engaged.

Self-Concept Versus Self-Esteem

Not long ago our doorbell rang, and as I answered it, I was surprised and happy to see a young lady (I'll call her Carol) who had been in my ward over a decade ago. I had been a bishop then, and she was an early teenager. Now in her late twenties, she was just as beautiful as she had been years earlier—only there was something missing.

Giving each other a warm embrace, I welcomed her into the house, and we spent the next hour getting caught up on each other's lives. She indicated that things had not gone well for her since we had last been in touch, and that she had given birth to a baby boy out of wedlock. I was very saddened to learn of this, especially since I remembered how spiritually inclined she had been, and how many commitments she had made to the Lord, years earlier.

We visited for a while longer, she showed me a photo of her beautiful son, and then we went right to the heart of why she had come to see me. She explained that she owned and operated a successful retail store in our community and that professionally things couldn't be going better. She likewise indicated that, even though her "spiritual dues" had been hard to pay, she had been meeting with her bishop for the previous year and had climbed out of the immoral relationship that had so devastated her. In fact, only weeks earlier she had been taken "off probation" by her caring bishop. Still, she said, she was a basket case and felt terrible about herself.

I should insert here that this young lady, if given the chance, could have entered the Miss America pageant four or five years earlier—she was *that* beautiful. However, she had begun eating the wrong foods, had put on an extra twenty to thirty pounds during her pregnancy, and had not gotten back to her original weight.

We then spent several moments talking about self-concept and self-esteem. I explained to her that our self-concept is *who* we think we are. In Carol's case, she knew she was a good mother; having a keen business sense, she knew she could provide financially for her small family; and she knew she had worked extremely hard to regain her spiritual footing and be worthy once again to partake of the sacrament.

Still, something very significant was missing in Carol's emotional makeup. She felt that life had passed her by, that she was not worthy to lose weight and be her beautiful self, and that no good returned missionary would want to marry her. In short, her self-esteem was extremely low.

Our self-concept, then, is *who we think we are.* Our self-esteem, on the other hand, is *how we feel about* who we think we are. These concepts are related but not necessarily the same. Let's explore them a little more deeply.

Sharlene Wells—Miss America, for Reals

Way back in 1983, I received an unexpected phone call. It was from the coordinator of judges for the Miss Utah pageant, and they still needed one judge to complete the panel of five judges necessary for their approaching pageant. I knew they were dipping into the bottom of the barrel for a final judge, as I had never even *attended* a pageant, let alone judged one. Even so, I felt that my experience as a seminary and institute instructor, as well as a marriage and family therapist, somewhat qualified me for the job. The good thing for them was that they didn't pay the judges to come and participate, so I figured they would be getting their money's worth out of my efforts. So, thinking this would be a unique opportunity, I quickly accepted.

The weekend for the pageant finally arrived, and as my wife and children took up residence at a local motel, then took over the motel swimming pool, I began an extraordinary three days. As I remember, there were over sixty contestants, each young lady filled with hopes and dreams. I knew that their parents would be popping their buttons with pride, since their beautiful and well-prepared daughters had won preliminary pageants in order to qualify for this one.

On the first day of events, we spent much of the day interviewing each of these young ladies. They were sharp, too, and seemed to be filled with a healthy self-concept as well as a good dose of self-esteem. One young lady especially impressed me, however, with her obvious self-confidence and articulate nature. Her name was Sharlene Wells, and she had won the Miss Salt Lake County pageant as her ticket to be there at that time.

In posing questions to Sharlene, each of the judges sensed there was just a little something extra in the way she responded. She didn't answer the questions any better than the others did, but she just had an additional *something* that caught my attention. Whoever Sharlene was, I knew how she felt about herself. I was convinced that she knew who she was and that she liked what she saw each morning as she looked into her bathroom mirror.

The pageant continued to unfold, and finally, during the last evening of competition, Sharlene won second runner-up to Miss Utah. She was only eighteen at the time, and was very pleased that she had done so well. In speaking with her afterward, I was especially impressed with how other-oriented she was in just wanting to talk about the young lady who had won the crown. That was unusual!

Later that night, as I was visiting with my wife, Margaret, back at our motel, I indicated to her that I felt Sharlene had the potential of becoming Miss America, even though she would not be going to Atlantic City that fall. She agreed, and so I called the other judges and arranged for us all to meet the following morning.

Sure enough, at 9:00 sharp, all the judges were sitting in a conference room at the motel, waiting to hear what I had to say. After I expressed my hopes for Sharlene's potential as a Miss America candidate, the judges gave their total support. Brainstorming together, we itemized nine areas that Sharlene could work on during the following year that would help her as she once again attempted to qualify for the Miss Utah pageant.

When we returned to our home in Salt Lake City, we called Sharlene and I expressed a desire to meet with her. Her mother was escorting Sharlene's younger sister, Elayne, at the America Junior Miss pageant (Elayne, as I recall, won second runner-up); and so Sharlene and her father, Elder Robert E. Wells of the First Quorum of the Seventy, came to my office the following Tuesday.

As the three of us sat down to visit, Sharlene indicated that she thought that perhaps she had participated in her last beauty pageant and that she wanted to prepare for a full-time mission. That was typical Sharlene—always thinking of ways she could serve!

I remember turning to her father and saying, "Elder Wells, what if becoming Miss America *is* Sharlene's mission? The judges all think she has the potential, and she can leave her destiny in the hands of the Lord."

Elder Wells, following his own impressions, quickly agreed.

In his own "unbiased" way, he could see that Sharlene did have this unusual potential.

I then surprised Sharlene by extracting a small white piece of paper from my pocket and handing it to her. "Here," I smiled, "take this. It is a list of nine 'areas of improvement' the judges feel you could work on as you prepare to enter the Miss Utah pageant next year. The judges won't be the same in next year's pageant, of course, for they can't judge pageants two years in a row. But, if you are who we each think you are, then you have a real shot at winning it!"

Sharlene hesitantly accepted the piece of paper and began to read the list. I don't recall all nine items, but I do recall four: *(1) Sing, as well as play the Paraguayan harp.* She had played only her instrument the previous night, but she had such a stunning voice, the audience deserved to hear her sing, even as she played. *(2) Wear a slightly more modest bathing suit—one that reflects your spiritual values.* Sharlene was a member of the Church, of course, but had simply purchased the most modest suit she could find. Now she would have to become creative, since modest bathing suits simply weren't to be found. *(3) Tone up your muscles more, so that when you are walking across the stage the judges can see how physically fit you are.* Sharlene had been an active basketball and track star in high school, and so I knew this would not be difficult for her to accomplish. *(4) Wear an evening gown that is of a color that allows your skin color to project into the audience.* She had worn a beautiful green gown the night before, but this color had not allowed her own color to project as well as it could have.

Well, we talked through these items, as well as the other five, and within minutes Sharlene and her father were out the door, and she was on her way to destiny.

I didn't hear from Sharlene after that meeting, but I was elated a year later to learn that she had very handily won the crown of Miss Utah. Three months later, after learning that she had won the swimsuit competition at the Miss America pageant in Atlantic City, I called her hotel to congratulate her.

When I called, Sharlene was back in her room, visiting with her mother. In congratulating her for winning this competition, I knew she had become physically fit and had looked good in her bathing suit. I asked her where she had purchased the suit, and she said simply, "Well, a very nice lady in Provo made one for me." That meant that she hadn't worn one with a French cut but rather had presented herself as being true to her acknowledged value system. The judges all knew she was a Latter-day Saint, and her suit reflected this fact. She told me that one of the reporters afterward had asked her how she could participate in a swimsuit competition, given her conservative religious values. She related to me that she simply smiled and said, "Our Church leaders counsel us to be physically fit, and in this competition I was showing that taking care of our bodies is something we should all make a priority in our lives." Enough said.

Two nights later, as our family watched Sharlene win the national title and be crowned Miss America for 1984, I waited for a couple of hours, then called her room. Again she was there, enjoying this most unlikely moment with her family. She didn't want to talk about the pageant, however, even though she was proud of her accomplishment. What she did want to talk about was the fact that she had given out two copies of the Book of Mormon to other contestants and that they were both interested in learning more about the Church! Again, vintage Sharlene—always looking beyond herself and desiring to serve others.

Throughout the next year, as again and again Sharlene was interviewed as the reigning Miss America, my wife and I noticed that she never focused on herself; rather, she would attempt to build others and to inspire the young people in the country to "realize their full potential."

Reflecting back on this singular experience, I honestly feel that I was "planted" among the other judges—all professional—so that I could be Sharlene's advocate for the following year. Not surprisingly, I have not been invited to judge a pageant since then. What I have done, though, is observe Sharlene as she has gone on to become a spokesperson for ESPN, as well as for the

Church, and a devoted wife and mother. She is definitely a person with a good self-concept, and she has allowed "keeping the commandments" to become her theme. This, in turn, has given her a healthy dose of self-esteem.

Les Misérables

Victor Marie Hugo was born in Besancon, France, in 1802. This was three years before Joseph Smith was born in Sharon, Vermont. When Napoleon seized control of France in 1851, Hugo was driven into exile to Brussels, then to the Channel Islands. Here he remained for nearly twenty years, until 1870. During this exile, which was for political reasons, Hugo wrote extensively and completed his most famous work, *Les Misérables.* The eagerly awaited book was published in 1862 throughout Europe and also in America. By the end of the 1800s, about seven million copies of the novel had been sold.

Anyway, in *Les Misérables,* which presents a fictitious setting for the infamous French Revolution, Hugo stated that most people spend their entire lives in quiet desperation. Think about it. That's quite a profound statement, and one that may not be that far off base. Most people spend their entire lives in quiet desperation.

As I have analyzed why this statement might be true, I have concluded it is because of people's low self-esteem. In diving deeper to analyze why people live with low self-esteem, I have concluded that it is because their behavior and their values are not aligned. That is, they believe certain things, yet don't match these values with how they behave. This, in turn, makes them most miserable—thus fulfilling the tragic state so poignantly presented by Victor Hugo.

And so if you are one who is living with a knot in the pit of your stomach as you are quietly and desperately struggling to be happy, let me suggest that you examine your values and your behavior. From my experience, and from what I have observed in others, we become "happy campers" only when these two areas of our lives are aligned.

Becoming Proactive

Not long ago, in an attempt to analyze what makes people of all ages happy, I met with two friends, Steve Swanson and Ron Newsom. During the course of our conversation, Ron outlined on a blackboard ways that people respond to life. In essence, he suggested that people—young and old alike—live either *proactively* or *reactively.*

When Ron first said these words, a light went on in my mind, and I could see why so many of those I had professionally counseled were so unhappy. I especially thought of the young people I knew and how so many of them simply "reacted" to life rather than approaching it positively, and with control.

We then spent the next couple of hours outlining a statement that shows the contrast between a person who is in a proactive mode and one who is in a reactive mode. Whether you are fifteen years old and anticipating your very first date or in your early twenties and reflecting on years of dating, these behavior modes are relevant to you.

The following statement reflects the things we discussed at that time:

Being Proactive Versus Being Reactive

I. When we are being proactive we do things because we want to. When we are being reactive, however, we do things because we have to.

II. When we are being proactive we focus on others. However, when we are being reactive we are very self-absorbed.

Being Proactive		*Being Reactive*
1. Being "in control."	vs.	1. Being "out of control." This person (a) becomes hysterical, (b) freezes, (c) escapes, or (d) tries to control others.

Being Proactive		*Being Reactive*
2. Being creative or alive.	vs.	2. Being first a victim, then an abuser.
3. Lots of options of things to do (new horizons).	vs.	3. No options. "I am stuck; can't see where to go."
4. Willing to take risks. Without risk there is no growth.	vs.	4. Taking no risk.
5. Self-validating.	vs.	5. Needing to seek validation or approval from others.
6. I accept myself and others.	vs.	6. I disqualify myself and others. When someone compliments me, I say, "No, I'm not really _______."
7. No justification, just action. I don't justify my behavior; I choose my behavior.	vs.	7. I justify and rationalize my choices.
8. Truth—I am truthful.	vs.	8. I choose to lie and deceive.
9. I do things now.	vs.	9. I procrastinate.

As you examine and contrast these two modes of behavior, you will quickly see which category you fall into. As a teenager, you probably see yourself becoming reactive with your parents when they don't see things as you do. You might also become reactive with your brothers and sisters, as well as close friends who may do something that betrays your relationship. Or, if you are in a dating relationship that seems to be "short circuiting," both you and your partner are likely beginning to react negatively to the other. The difficult result of your behaving in this mode is that you spin out of control and become extremely unhappy.

Let me now give you a challenge. Mark this page in your book, then reread it once or twice a day for a couple of weeks. As you do you will soon internalize its contents, and then when a "reactive moment" presents itself, you can quickly identify it as such, then respond from a proactive perspective. This information could be one of the most crucial learning tools you will ever receive, so good luck in becoming a proactive person!

The Law of the Fence

Growing up in rural Nephi, Utah, gave my brothers and me the "opportunity" to be assigned a cow to milk, feed, and watch over. Her name was Hepsibah, although we affectionately called her simply Hepsi. Now, Hepsi was a good cow, as cows go, even though we felt tremendously picked on by our dad (especially when we became very handsome and athletic teens) to have to milk her—and to feed and water her—twice a day.

One morning, when Hepsi was feeling particularly adventurous, she noticed a weakness in our fence. Within minutes she had worked her way through the fence and was eating away at our alfalfa field. As I recall, she ate so much of this "delicious green stuff" that she bloated up and became very ill.

The veterinarian, Mr. Memmott, came and attended to her, thus saving her life. Still, after that, things never were the same for Hepsi. She would literally poke at every part of the fence until she found a loose area to climb through. Finally, in an attempt to teach her not to escape, Dad hooked up a battery to the top wire in the fence and made it electrically charged. Then, whenever Hepsi had her wandering notions, she would nudge her nose up against the fence and receive the intended shock. That electric shock would frighten her, and she would then back away from the fence.

As I look back on this incident, I think of each of us and how tempting it is for us to try to escape the fences that our parents enclose around us. The grass really does seem greener on the other side, and whether it is whom we associate with, the time we are expected in at night, the frequency of dating a particular person, or whatever, the fences that have been established are for our good, and our spiritual protection.

Now for the Law of the Fence.

Perhaps you have heard the poem about how we live on the edge of a cliff and have either an ambulance waiting for us down in the valley—for when we fall off the cliff—or fences built that keep us from wandering dangerously close to the edge of the cliff in the first place. In the latter case, with many fences built, we pretty much eliminate the need for maintaining the ambulance way down in the valley. We simply won't be dangling our feet out over the crags of the cliff.

So it is with life. Those who walk out to the edge, then dangle their feet out in the air, have a pretty good chance of losing their balance and falling. They risk their safety by not attending church or by developing distance in their relationship with their parents. They also do it by going with only one person, thereby increasing their chances of falling prey to premarital sexual intimacy; or by associating with those who don't value living the Word of Wisdom and other teachings of the Church.

On the other hand, there are those young people who are wise beyond their years. I know, for I have taught them, and have even seen them in my own children. These people awaken each morning, build another fence of protection from Satan's crags and cliffs, and then enjoy the peace and safety of spending that day on solid ground.

I have actually identified five areas—types of fences, if you will—that can provide the protection you will need at this precarious moment in your life to keep you away from the dangers of the cliff. They are as follows:

1. Be a hundred-percenter in your church attendance. Never sleep in or have other activities take priority over attending the full three-hour block of meetings.

2. Have a personal devotional each day (either at the beginning of your day or at the end). Read at least one chapter in the Book of Mormon. Then, after reading, kneel down and offer a totally sincere prayer to Heavenly Father.

3. Pay a full and honest tithe, and do so when you first receive a paycheck. In addition, rejoice in paying it! The Lord will truly shower blessings down upon you.

4. Be (or become) totally morally clean. This includes personal cleanliness, as well as relationship cleanliness. We will discuss this more in a later chapter.

5. Become and then remain temple worthy. If you are endowed, then keep your temple recommend current. If not, then be temple worthy by doing baptisms for the dead and by honorably answering worthiness questions asked by your bishop.

I have honestly found that those young people who do these five things, or who build these five fences, almost float into the temple when it is time for them to marry. That is, they don't spend months and years in repentance programs, after slipping on the jagged edges of the cliff, but remain free of that. Instead, they are able to enjoy the Light of Christ and have the blessings and companionship of the Holy Spirit, and they can then reach out to others in a caring, serving manner.

Now, for the exciting part: If you are ready to incorporate these fences in your life, you may want to do so by fasting and prayer. Make a commitment to the Lord that you will do these things, and these commitments can aid you in keeping your covenants. You know what those are for you made covenants, or promises, with the Lord at the time you were baptized. You promised that you would take upon yourself the Savior's name (that is, acknowledge yourself as a true Christian), that you would remember his life and his atonement, and that you would keep each of his commandments—not just those that are convenient to keep, but all of them. These are the things you should be thinking about each week as you renew your baptismal covenants by partaking of the Lord's sacrament.

Promising to keep the commandments and then keeping them will help you develop your character. I define character as a person's ability to sustain a decision long after the moment of making that decision has passed. If you are attempting to become a young man or woman of character, make this decision and then live by it! You will be amazed at how much power such a commitment will give you.

The Lord has promised that, as you keep your promises to him, you will have his Spirit with you on a constant basis. In other words, you will have an automatic insulation from the wiles of the devil, and you will have greater power to do what you have promised you will do.

In conclusion, then, we have talked about several principles in this chapter that, if incorporated in your life, will measurably increase your happiness. These are:

1. Enhance your self-esteem—how you feel about yourself.
2. Become the very best you can be. Realize your personal potential.
3. Live your life proactively, not reactively.
4. Live the law of the fence. Protect yourself against the dangers of the adversary.
5. Honor your baptismal covenants. Be a true follower of Christ.

With this foundation let us now begin to explore the wild and zany dating scene of the 1990s. Kick back, be happy you're not out on a date this very evening, and read about some of the perils and pleasures of dating.

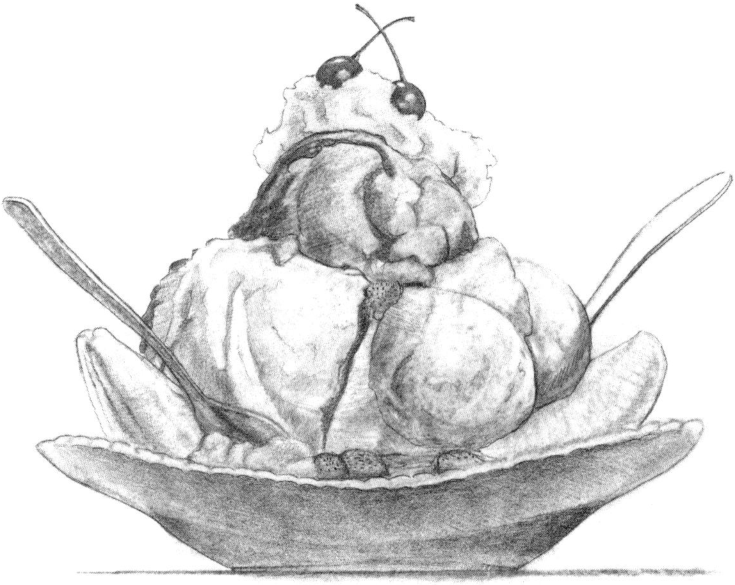

3

The Fun and Frenzy of Casual Dating

Albert Einstein said this: "When you sit with a nice girl for two hours, you think it's only a minute. But, when you sit on a hot stove for a minute, you think it's two hours. That's relativity!"

I can think of few experiences more gratifying for you than to be able to spend time with someone of the opposite sex—someone you have special feelings toward. Likewise, I can't think of anything more uncomfortable than to see you with someone you clash with.

In chapter 1, we enjoyed the humorous though uncomfortable first date between a fictional Tausha and Josh. Both were unsure of themselves, yet they had great expectations for the feelings they were having about each other. Such ambivalence of feelings is not unusual—regardless of how old you are and how seasoned you are as a dating partner. Breaking the ice is a difficult experience, regardless of the circumstance, and each partner should do what he or she can to make things easier for the other.

Dating Trends

The phenomenon of dating is actually very recent in our society. It emerged in the 1920s, following World War I. Prior to that time, couples "sparked and spooned" and certainly paired off; but it was not in a formal dating manner. Now, however, three-quarters of a century later, the experience of dating is alive and doing well.

In many ways, actually, dating has come full circle. In the early teen years, and then later into the college-age years, individuals are engaging more and more in group dating. Instead of pairing off, friends of both sexes are spending platonic evenings enjoying each other's company without the entanglements of romance. As a father of nine—six of whom have reached the ripe old dating age of sixteen—I have been delighted and amazed at how many times our children have chosen to be with groups rather than pairing off with one other person.

On one occasion I overheard our seventeen-year-old daughter turn down a date. She told the fellow, "My friends and I already have something planned for that evening, so I can't go with you." After she hung up the phone, I asked her why in the world she would turn this fellow down for a date. After all, she had indicated that he was an "awesome, dripping hunk" that she hoped to one day go out with. She was very sincere in telling me how much fun she and her friends had as they went western line dancing at Wheeler Farm. So much for pairing-off priorities for her!

Still, casual and serious dating trends are well entrenched in our society, with each partner having expectations of a pleasurable evening for themselves, as well as for their partner. Even though you have likely "bombed out" with a date that just didn't work, there are several reasons why you have not given up but have kept going back for more.

First, you date because you want to have fun and enjoy social experiences. Although it is not something you often think about, dating also affords the opportunity for you both to experience personal development. Personal growth can occur as you make mistakes, then as you suffer and make amends for what you have said or done, and finally as you apologize and learn from what has happened. How many times have you said something like,

"Boy, I sure blew it! He (or she) will never talk to me again. I'll never be dumb enough to do that again." Do these statements sound familiar? They do to me, even though it has been nearly three decades since I was in the dating scene.

As you move through your teen years, and as your relationships mature, you will want to date only the type of person who is a potential marriage partner. That doesn't mean that you change the type of person you go out with, but that you begin to go out only with individuals who present themselves as "marriage material." This occurs when you are tired of the dating game and you begin to date primarily to select a marriage partner.

I recall that following my mission I began a serious quest of dating only those young ladies who had "marriage potential." Although I didn't have instant success (I dated over thirty girls before I met my future mate), I kept after it—and rarely did a week pass that I did not go on at least one or two dates. My wife actually went on a mission the month I returned from my mission, and although we didn't meet until two months after her return, this time of steady dating (not going steady) was definitely one of relationship growth for me.

Costs of Dating

Although we usually like to talk only about the benefits of dating, there are also certain costs associated with this phenomenon that you should consider. One of these costs is actually *not* dating. Many young people of both sexes develop severe inferiority complexes when they do not date. This usually takes place more with young ladies, as we live in a society where the young men do most of the asking. There are times, however, when young men do not ask someone out, simply because they lack the self-confidence to do so.

Some time ago a former student came to my home and was extremely depressed. After shedding a half bucket of tears, she finally cleared her throat enough to speak. She literally blurted out the following: "Why don't I ever date? I don't think I'm really bad-looking, yet I haven't had even one date in my entire high school career!"

I seriously considered skirting the issue for my friend, for fear of hurting her self-esteem even more. Truth prevailed, however, as I decided to risk my relationship with this young lady. I told her that during the two years I had known her, I had never seen her wear a dress. Her hair was unkempt, and she wore no makeup. I suggested that she would begin to be treated like a young lady when she began to look and act like one.

At first this young lady pouted and explained away her appearance; but after a few moments she acknowledged her slothfulness, then resolved to become more feminine in appearance. Would you believe that only weeks later she was asked out? She won, and today she is happily married. In fact, I saw her not long ago, when I was purchasing a car. Her husband was with her, and she was proud as punch to show him off to me.

One of the other costs of dating is the possibility that it can actually impair personal growth. I know this seems impossible, but it happens when one or both partners play a game and don't allow themselves to speak truth in the things they are saying to each other on their dates. This can happen when there is an emphasis on appearance, superficial social skills, and small talk.

As long as you use "fronts," rather than developing your real self, you are limiting and likely damaging your personal growth. If, however, you focus on important values and interests, you will gradually wean yourself away from playing the dating game.

Understanding Desired Dating Roles

One of the most difficult aspects of dating is understanding the set of roles that both young men and young women identify as being proper or appropriate in various dating situations. Young ladies are especially concerned about this, since one mistake may mean the end of a relationship. One of my students, who was vitally concerned with this problem, wrote the following poem:

We Can't Win

If a girl speaks to a boy, she's forward;
If she doesn't, she's bashful.
If she talks to a boy, she's a flirt;
If she doesn't, she's shy.
If she's smart in school, she's a sissy;
If she isn't, she's dumb.
If she talks about others, she's catty;
If she doesn't, she doesn't get along with others.
If she goes out with many boys, she's a pick-up;
If she doesn't, she's a wallflower.
If she's popular, she becomes an item of gossip;
If she isn't, she's ignored.
If she wears a boy's ring, she stole it;
If she doesn't, she couldn't get one.
If she tints her hair, she's cheap;
If she doesn't, she's chicken.
If she dances with younger guys, she's robbin' the cradle;
If she doesn't, she has no school spirit.

—Barbara Horton

As you may suspect, defining acceptable patterns of behavior is no easy task. If you want to know what type of person you are or how you come across to your partner on a date, answer the following questionnaire:

Girls: Answer for yourselves
Boys: Answer the way you want a girl to answer

(Please answer Yes *or* No*)*

1. Do you like to always be in control on a date?
2. Are you inwardly happy when your date is happy?
3. Do you want to marry only a potentially successful person?
4. Do you enjoy being near your date?

5. Do you prefer being independent, not having to depend on your date?
6. Do you admire your date?
7. Do you often reprimand your date for misbehavior?
8. Do you want to be tenderly cared for by your date?
9. Are you cautious on dates?
10. Do you dress to suit your date?
11. Do you stay at least one step ahead of your date?
12. Are you disturbed if your date is disturbed at you?
13. Do you wish you could stay at least one step ahead of your date?
14. Do you allow your date to make the decisions on the dates?
15. Do you subtly manipulate your date?
16. Do you accept your date's criticisms?
17. Do you try to make all the decisions on dates?
18. Would you ever go stag to a party?

You will be interested to know that, if you are a girl, you have just identified yourself as being either assertive or receptive. If you are a boy, you have just expressed your preference for dating an assertive or a receptive girl. Here's the definition of each of these two personality types:

Assertive. A person who is achievement oriented, who dominates, who can be quite hostile, who is a status aspirant or a status driver. An assertive person is one who takes the initiative or acts as an aggressor in most dating activities.

Receptive. A person who is deferential (enjoys caring for her date), who is prone to vicariousness (lives in a dream world), who is a hero worshipper, and who is responsive in most dating activities to male initiative.

Now return to the questions. Add up all of the even-numbered questions you answered with a yes, and add up all of the odd-numbered questions you answered with a yes. Responding with a yes to most of the odd-numbered questions indicates that you are assertive if you are a girl, or that you prefer an assertive companion if you are a boy. On the other hand, if the majority of the yeses fall on the even-numbered questions, you are receptive or you prefer dating girls who have a receptive nature. This exercise should enable you to learn a little more about your own personality, as well as what you desire in dating relationships.

What Color Are You?

One of my dear friends and neighbors is Dr. Taylor Hartman. In his profession as a therapist, he classifies people into four personality types. He uses the colors of red, blue, white, and yellow as symbols to identify our motives and to determine what motivates us to behave the way we do. To allow you to examine yourself from what he calls the "Color Code," the following description of each "color" is adapted from Dr. Hartman's book of that title (Taylor Don Hartman, 1987, pp. 17–21):

Reds: These people are hungry for power and want their own way. They like to work and often are called workaholics. They like to appear knowledgeable and crave approval from others for their intelligence and insight. Reds want to be respected more than they want to be loved, and they seek leadership opportunities.

Blues: These people crave intimacy in relationships. They love to do things for others and have a strong need to be loved. They need tender loving care. They also have a very strong moral conscience and enjoy being "good." They have a very strong sense of integrity and would rather lose than cheat.

Whites: These people are motivated by peace. They will do almost anything to avoid confrontation. They like to "go with the flow" in relationships, and *feeling* good is even more important to them than *being* good. Whites need kindness, and they like to keep a low profile. They are independent people and are motivated by other people's desires.

Yellows: These people are motivated by having fun. They consider life to be a daily party. They welcome praise, need intimacy, want to be popular, and like adventure and action. You can never be bored around a Yellow personality, because they are having too much fun!

An interesting observation, and perhaps the very key to understanding your personality, is that your motive, and not your behavior, determines your primary personality. Now that you know this, read back through these four core personality types and see what motivates you. Learning what color you are, and what types of people you like to date, can be very helpful in your dating selections.

Dating Values and Rewards

Dating is a learned behavior. It is not just something we intuitively know how to do. However, you actually begin learning how to date much earlier than your first dating experience, since you learn dating rules from parents, older brothers and sisters, and others in your own peer group. You also learn how to date from television shows, music videos, CD's, books, and so forth.

Since 1990s dating involves a significant investment of money, time, and personal talents and capabilities, it should have some value and rewards. The process of asking someone out becomes almost as expensive and time-consuming as the date itself—and it becomes a rewarding and exciting experience of its own.

One morning five young men showed up on our doorstep, unannounced, and asked to spread Jolly Rancher candies all over the bed of our seventeen-year-old daughter, Jennifer. We complied, and soon the candy was spread, surrounding a large poster board that said this: "Jen—Hey, sweet [peach], I'd be a Jolly Rancher if you'd go to the theme dance with me February 25th. The Jolly Ranchers hold my identity!" Where the poster said *peach,* there was a real peach. Spread across the poster, and all over the bed, were several dozen Jolly Ranchers. Inside one of these, of course, was the identity of the young man asking her out. Talk about an investment of time and money—just to ask her out!

And so, with so much time and energy as well as money invested, dates should be a meaningful venture in personal relationships between a boy and a girl. On a date you can plan on having a good time regardless of what you are doing—if both of you share the responsibility of making the evening enjoyable and your relationship at least respectful. Too often one partner or both have a miserable experience, simply because they transfer the responsibility of having a good time to the other person. This same person often shifts the blame for an unpleasant date onto the shoulders of his or her dating partner.

Bonds of Attachment

You will come to appreciate that even though you will marry only one of your dating partners, many of the others you date will eventually become your lifelong friends. As you date these people, you will find a bond of attachment developing between you and at least some of these partners. This is not an unbreakable trust, but it is a significant feeling of confidence. Then, as your dating becomes more frequent and you begin to share values, it becomes easier for your relationship to encompass other expressions of trust and security.

Still, let me say something more about the natural bonds of attachment you develop with certain meaningful dating partners. As a marriage counselor I have met many people who look back to meaningful dating partners that they did not marry—and they feel guilt for the feelings of love and attachment they still experience for those partners. This is very tragic, for a person can't simply announce that she is erasing her feelings toward another person just because she didn't choose to marry that person. Bonds of attachment don't simply go away because you stop dating someone. To the contrary, they may last a lifetime, or at least years into your marriage with someone else. The healthy thing for you to know at this time is that these bonding emotions gradually shift from romantic feelings to platonic emotions.

Now, let us continue our discussion of dating.

Dating can also be a special way of getting to know and understand yourself as well as your dating partners. I think it is exciting that dating allows you the opportunity to broaden and deepen your perspectives.

Dating for Group Status

One of the basic needs which dating satisfies for you is that of group status. My wife and I both remember that during our dating days it was vitally important for us to know that we had status within our respective groups; and this was achieved largely through our dating experiences. Have you ever considered that dating is actually a group activity, even though the interaction occurs between you and your partner? This is true because you must abide by the rules set by your group if you wish to retain status in your group.

Group status, and group reliance, is especially important during the early dating years. When you are older, however, it takes on less importance as you date in hopes of finding your eternal mate. This fact was brought again to my attention when our eldest son came home from college. He was home only for an hour because he had a very special date lined up. When I asked him if it was a group date or a single date, he simply said, "Well, there are three couples planning on going, which will be good because this is a first date for me. However, if the others aren't able to make it, I'll still have a great time with my date. It's really okay either way."

Although the dating spectrum extends from a person's earliest dating experiences to the serious process of mate selection, our discussion at this time is limited to the uncommitted form of dating. This is called casual dating and is the opposite of going steady. The essence of casual dating is to play the field far and wide, and to date as many partners as one can. The objective is to have fun, to explore personalities, and to get to know yourself as well as those you date.

In your teen years, especially, there are several advantages to dating a variety of partners. For one thing, it keeps you from getting tied down and becoming obligated to any one girl or boy. Not only is it an exciting way of circulating and getting to know many members of the opposite sex, but it also allows you to broaden your own personality as you explore and realize your own potential. It may also be true that having many dating partners is flattering to the ego—a way of enhancing one's feelings of self-worth.

Apples Versus Oranges

As you reflect upon what you read in the previous paragraph, perhaps it would be well to consider the similarity principle of mate selection. This is where "like marries like." It is actually called the homogamy theory of selecting a mate. The notion is that we should date many people so that we can find how similar we are to them. Similarity is important in two areas—values and role expectations. A value might be expressed in how important church attendance is, or how important a temple marriage is. A role expectation, on the other hand, might be reflected in whether you want a small or large family, or whether you both feel the same about the wife having a profession that takes her out of the home.

In these instances, like really should marry like. For discussions of such matters, I sometimes compare people to types of fruit. I tell young people that apples should marry apples, watermelons should marry watermelons, and pomegranates should marry pomegranates. The more similar you are in values and role expectations, the more likely you will be to have a happy and fulfilling marriage.

Did you know that if you were to marry today, and both you and your partner were out of your teens, you would still have only a fifty-fifty chance of having your marriage work? If, on the other hand, you are both still in your teens (and you don't know if you are an orange, or a grape, or something else and you don't know what your partner is either), your chance of experiencing divorce is six times greater than before. Therefore, if you marry in your teen years, you have about a five or six percent chance of having your marriage succeed.

As you contemplate these statistics, you can see why your parents encourage you to group date, and to casual date, while you are in your teens—so that you won't make the mistake of marrying the wrong type of person for you. This is a very important thought for you to consider.

The Dating Dilemma

One thing which contributes to frustration on dates is not knowing what to do or where to go. This is less crucial in larger cities, where there are so many options for dating. Still, I have included the following ideas for you to consider, if you need suggestions of things to do on dates:

Dating in Grubbies

Go western line dancing
Go skydiving (if your parents will allow you to!)
Go for a bike ride up the canyon and have a picnic
Go horseback riding and play cops and robbers
Have a dog wash—wash the neighborhood dogs
Go rabbit hunting
Go sand jumping
Go ice skating or roller skating
Go to an amusement park
Go to a water slide or a water theme park
Swing at the park
Visit your state capitol or your favorite community attractions
Go mountain climbing
Have a water-balloon fight
Go glacier sliding
Race toy trains
Build a dam in a stream or gutter
Ride a jeep to the top of a mountain and cook dinner or have a picnic

Paint a barn or a house
Fly paper airplanes
Make mud pies and have a fight
In a group, take an after-dark hike with flashlights
Go bug collecting up the canyon
Take a sunrise hike and cook breakfast afterwards
Go graveyard walking
Go snipe hunting
Play in a fountain
Go on a scavenger hunt
Go skateboard riding
Go skiing or snowboarding
Go river running
Play hopscotch in a parking lot
Have a house-cleaning party
Have a lawn-mowing and garage-cleaning party
Wash each other's cars
Rent motorcycles or go four-wheeling
Go on a hayride
Go to a wooded area and build a Robinson Crusoe hut
Play cowboys and Indians
Look for things at the city dump
Go caving and exploring
Go fly a kite
Have a food or pie fight
Climb trees
Roll down hills
Go frog catching and have a frog jumping contest
Do a craft—make candles, macrame, finger paint
Ride the train at the zoo—have a picnic
Take bikes in a car to the top of a mountain, then ride down
Play croquet in the dark, using flashlights
Get ice blocks and slide down grassy hills
Use a truck and set up a table in the back, then have a tail-gate dinner (Do this at a drive-in or a parking lot)

Informal Dating

Visit Temple Square or the visitors' center of your nearest temple
Rent a truck or moving van and have a party in it
Have a candlelight dinner in the mountains, at a parking terrace, etc.
Pick up date, go to a movie, then window-shop—all without the use of a car
Take sightseeing tour of city on a bus
Go elevator shopping
Visit a fish hatchery
Play bird-watching at the aviary
Ride the Heber Valley Railroad (or visit another local attraction)
Cook dinner together
Go to a planetarium
Go to an outdoor symphony concert
Go to a melodrama or to a small theater in the round
Fix popcorn and watch a classic scary movie
Visit the wax museum
Walk in the rain, fog, or snow
Visit travel agencies and plan a trip
Walk through Memory Grove and visit Charlie's Bench (in Salt Lake City)
Go on the merry-go-round at a park
Go antique hunting
Go to the library, watch a video, or listen to music
Have a banana-split-making contest
Shop for diamonds at jewelry stores
See what kind of good deed you can do for a quarter
Tour any historical sites in your area
Visit a homeless shelter and give them some homemade cookies
Tour a mortuary
Visit a rest home with treats for the residents
Buy ingredients and cook dinner for fifty cents a person

Dressy

Go to breakfast in dinner clothes
Have a progressive dinner
Go to a hamburger drive-in in formal attire
Go to a play or symphony
Boys cook a formal dinner for girls or vice versa
Have a chauffeur and red carpet treatment for dinner

Miscellaneous

Ask a date by postcard or any unusual way: puzzle, cookie hunt, etc.
Play hide and seek in a department store
Play jacks or Risk at the airport
Have a birthday party for anyone, use strange utensils
Have a backwards party—menus, clothes, etc., all backwards
Go to a hotel lobby and watch television
Weave baskets
"Kidnap" your date
Teach boys to make bread or a cake
Bottle fruit in the summer
Go Christmas caroling in August
Have an Easter egg roll on public building steps
Roast hot dogs on the most appropriate fire you can find
Go to a drive-in, taking brothers and sisters along
Build an igloo
Color in coloring books
Watch the planes or trains come in
Go to the drag or stock car races
Play kick the can
Go people watching and take notes
Sell bubblegum
Have an ice race with straws
Have a bubble-gum-blowing contest
Go to the county or state fair

Go waterskiing
Go wading in some unusual place
Get a team and play baseball, volleyball, etc., at night
Pop popcorn in the fireplace
Have a taffy pull
Go rowing or canoeing on the nearest lake
Tie a quilt
Make a home movie—write script, film, give academy awards
Visit a ghost town
Make treats and leave them on someone's doorstep

Use your imagination, get permission (parents, owners, etc.) and, above all, use good taste—don't do something against the law or at someone else's expense—and have a great time!

What "Turns You Off"?

The dating experience, with its high priority in your social life, contains trauma of many kinds. How to handle this trauma may be difficult to determine by two partners who are so involved in their relationship that they aren't able to "see the forest for the trees." Because of this, I include the following list of things you may be doing (heaven forbid!) or your partner may be doing (heaven forbid again!) that "bug" the other. Many of these things are trivial, but knowing one another's expectations about dating behavior may allow you to have more rewarding and enjoyable dating experiences.

Things that bother girls about what boys do on dates

Doesn't talk or carry on a conversation
Impolite, bad manners, won't open the door for you
Date isn't planned—boy doesn't make decision, but asks what you want to do
Aggressive, touchy
Talks about other girls

Insists on kissing
Shows off, sarcastic, big joker
Swears or profanes
Feels that he must spend money or eat
Puts on an act
Thinks he is greater than you
Cuts himself down
Stands too long on the porch and won't leave
Drives too fast
Gives other girls "the eye" on his date with you—flirts
Crude—burps, spits
Comes over with friends and whispers about you to them
Shy—won't touch you
Tries to impress you with his car
Complains about how expensive the date is
Stays out too late
Calls your girl friend to ask if you like him
Can't stand silence
Always takes you to the same types of activities
Takes your good friend out right after you stop going with him
Insists you sit next to him
Kisses you on the first date
Rude to you all during the date if you make one mistake
Doesn't ask you out after you have taken him out
Makes you order food first
Comes over to watch television—won't take you out
Insecure
Talks tough about drinking and smoking, or even using drugs
Leaves you alone and talks to his friends
Uses too much cologne
Doesn't shave
Too serious
Doubles with people you don't know
Wears clothes that don't go together
Expects a performance from you as payment for his taking you out

Has dirty fingernails
Doubles with other couples who are into "making out"
Thinks you have a crush on him if you say hi to him
Always single dates
Talks too much
Embarrassed when his friends see him with you
After going together once, he follows you everywhere and expects you to talk to him and be with him

Things that bother boys about what girls do on dates

Doesn't talk or carry on a conversation
Door hugger
Won't help make a decision on what to do—says, "I don't know"
Doesn't order dinner (says no to eating, but really is hungry)
Talks about other boys
She's not ready for the date when you come to pick her up
Acts like she is doing you a favor by going out with you
Gossips about you
Expects you to be with her all the time
On double dates, the girls talk to the girls, so the boys must talk to the boys
Gets uptight over little things
Forward
Flirts with other guys on a date or when she knows you're around
Says how fat or ugly she is
Acts dumb or bored
Wears excessive makeup
Likes you for your money or your car
Always asks what time it is
Leads you on
Runs to the door after a date
Fixes her hair in the car
Refuses to talk about herself

Asks if you are upset with her
Always going to the restroom
Wears too much perfume
Complains about this and that
Giggles all of the time
Worries about how her clothes look
Puts on an act
Talks altogether too much
She thinks she is a "mover"
Smoking, drinking, swearing
Wears the wrong clothes for the date
Goofs off in a restaurant
Won't let you help her with her coat
Thinks you like her for security
No dresses; always pants, pants, pants
Won't tell you if she doesn't like you
Has her friends ask if you like her
Expects fancy dates
Goes on a date not expecting to have fun

Many of the items shared on this list seem adolescent and immature—and they are! What's surprising to me is how many young men and women, even after they have "graduated" out of their teens, continue to behave in this manner. Hopefully, after reading through this list, you will mentally check the areas where you can improve. As a final thought, be kind and forgiving when those you date behave beneath *their* expectations of themselves.

4

Dating Questions and Quandaries

Once when I was discussing with a group of students in a dating and courtship class the ramifications of the dating game, one of them suggested that each member of the class write down his or her biggest hang-up about dating. Would you enjoy reading what your peers had to say? I have included their questions below and have then followed these questions with my answers.

Why is there such a big deal made about being sixteen years old before we can date? I think that perhaps the first thing to discuss is that it is not a matter of distrust to suggest that someone younger than age sixteen not be allowed to date. Rather, it is, in part, a concern that early dating may result in an early appetite for physical affection. For years, the General Authorities of the Church have counseled us not to date until we are at least sixteen years of age. A more recent statement, however, was issued in the pamphlet *For the Strength of Youth* in 1990, a publication printed at the request of and with the approval of the First Presidency and the Quorum of the Twelve. On page 7 we read:

Begin to prepare now for a temple marriage. Proper dating is a part of that preparation.

In cultures where dating is appropriate, do not date until you are sixteen years old. . . . Many young people do not date during their teen years, because they are not interested, do not have opportunities, or simply want to delay forming serious relationships. Good friendships can be developed at every age.

When you begin dating, go in groups or on double dates. Avoid pairing off exclusively with one partner. Make sure your parents meet and become acquainted with those you date. Later the time will come for choosing just one. You may occasionally want to invite your dates to activities with your family.

Plan positive and constructive activities when you are together. Do things that help you get to know each other. Be careful to go to places where there is a good environment, where you won't be faced with temptation.

Follow the Brethren Always

At this writing, six of our nine children have reached the ripe old age of sixteen. For each of them this has meant they have "come of age" and have been able to get their driver's license. Permit me to be personal (I have their permission) by sharing their individual experiences as they approached this magical age of dating.

Jason, our eldest, was one month away from turning sixteen. It was Halloween time and we as a family were returning to our home. As we pulled into the driveway, we noticed a giant pumpkin on the front porch. The kids all poured out of the van to see who had delivered such a gift. It was a very special girl in our ward, and she was a senior in high school. She was inviting Jason to the Halloween dance, and she asked him to respond by carving the pumpkin with a smile if the answer was yes and with a frown if the answer was no.

Jason had matured early, and was a six-foot-one-inch weight lifter; I'll never forget him looking down at me and asking honestly, "Dad, do we have a rule that we kids can't date until we're sixteen?"

I thought for a moment, then replied, "No, for as you know, our only rule is that there are no rules unless you break one!" We laughed, and then he asked the question again, very seriously.

This time I answered by saying, "Actually, Jase, we do have a guideline of not dating prior to age sixteen, as you know. Still, it is your decision. However, before you make it, let me share a thought. If you begin at age fifteen and eleven-twelfths to follow the Brethren all the time, then when you are twenty-five and fifty-five you will do the same thing—you will always do what the Brethren have asked you to do. If, however, you begin at this time to pick and choose which of their directives you are going to follow, then you will be picking and choosing for the rest of your life."

Jason thought for a moment, then said, "I guess I'll follow the Brethren all the time. But how do I get out of the date?"

"It's easy, Jase," I answered, obviously relieved by his decision. "Just carve the pumpkin with a smile on one side and a frown on the other. Take it to her with a note telling her that you'll take a rain check."

Jason did just that, and a few months later, long after his sixteenth birthday, he took this young lady to a priest/Laurel steak fry.

Fifteen months passed, and Aaron, our second son, was one month away from his sixteenth birthday. He came home from school and learned that he had been asked out by someone for the high school Valentine's Day dance. He asked me what he should do, and I simply said, "What did Jason do, Aaron, when this happened to him?"

"Well," Aaron smiled, remembering my earlier conversation with Jase, "he didn't go. Actually, I don't think I will, either. But how do I get out of it?"

"Just tell her you'll take a rain check," I answered, remembering how well the idea had worked for Jason. Aaron did this and stayed home until after his sixteenth birthday.

Fourteen months later our third son, Jeremy, came home and announced, "Dad, I've been grabbed!" He was literally one month away from *his* sixteenth birthday, and I didn't know what he meant by "being grabbed." I didn't know whether to be excited for him or to be concerned.

"What do you mean, Jer bud? What do you mean, you've 'been grabbed'?"

"Well, at school they have a Grab Dance. If a girl grabs you in the hall, then you have to take her to the dance that night. So, what do I do? I mean, I won't be sixteen for another month."

"What did your older brothers do, Jer, when this happened to them?"

Jeremy remembered well and recited their experiences. He also remembered what I had said about following the prophets, and he said, "I think I'll call her and tell her I can't go but that I'll take a rain check for when I'm old enough."

I was so proud of Jeremy that I gave him five dollars, and he and his fifteen-year-old buds went out for pizza. Each had likewise been "grabbed," and each had made the same decision as Jeremy. It was a great moment in our home, believe me!

Well, three years passed, and a month before our fourth son, Josh, turned sixteen, he came home and said, "Why hasn't anyone asked me out, Dad?"

We laughed, remembering the experiences of his elder brothers. Josh made it well past his sixteenth birthday before going on his first date.

Two years passed, and Jen, our eldest daughter, went out on her first date on her sixteenth birthday! Can you believe that? There was a good reason, though, and not one you would imagine. You see, her birthday was October twenty-ninth, the very day of the high school's Halloween dance. It was a girl's choice dance, as you remember from our eldest son's experience, and so she made sure that she went out. It was great!

Our sixth child, Don, likewise turned sixteen "without opportunity," and so we have been fortunate. Our kids are not perfect by any means, but it has been gratifying to see that even though they are human and make mistakes, they each want to follow the Brethren all the time.

How can you let a guy know you like him without chasing him away? One of the excitements of dating is also one of the hazards. Dating is truly a game, at least during the early stages of nonsteady dating. Girls have been struggling with this dilemma for many years, and boys have been exploiting their dilemma for the same period of time!

One of the patterns of early dating is the cat and mouse game. A boy will like a certain girl until he finds that she likes him, or vice versa. You should try not to come on too strong. First become friends, then allow that friendship to develop naturally. The most reassuring thing I can say is that when you grow older and begin dating for the purposes of selecting an eternal companion, you will find that your relationships last longer. They also become more meaningful and, consequently, become less of a game. In a mature relationship, however, both partners sense an excitement as well as a security in knowing the feelings each has for the other.

Should I kiss on the first date? When I was a teenager my father taught my siblings and me that a kiss was "an anatomical juxtaposition of two orbicularis muscles in contraction." We were pretty much heroes at school once we had memorized this cumbersome phrase and could then ask our classmates what it described. No one could guess, of course, and so when we would announce that it was a kiss, our memory (although likely inaccurate) is that they were impressed!

Thus, other than an "Aunt Polly peck," this was my first introduction to the expression of a kiss. Although I'm quite sure that we were taught the sacred nature of a kiss, I don't remember it. What I *do* remember is that kisses were given and received freely among my peers. Kissing was basically a social expression, with nothing sacred about it.

Following my full-time mission, as I began to date "for reals," I began to treat the kiss differently. In fact, I became so concerned about not overstepping my bounds that I literally asked my sweetheart's permission before I kissed her. Fortunately, she consented and we had a kiss that still lingers in my mind. This was the evening before I asked her to marry me.

And so, as young people growing up in a totally permissive society, I would ask you this: Do you feel that a kiss should be simply a routine social expression; or do you think it should be reserved and expressed only when feelings of love are growing within you?

I was once counseling a young lady who was well into her eighteenth year. She had dated regularly since age sixteen, yet had not allowed any of her dates to kiss her. She was a spectacularly beautiful young lady in every way and had earned her Young Womanhood Recognition award. When I asked her why she hadn't yet had her first kiss, she said simply, "Well, my parents taught me that kissing makes a girl common, and I can wait. After all, when I kiss someone I want to do it when our feelings have grown enough to have it mean something."

I congratulated this young lady for treating the kiss with such care. She, for one, determined that she would never kiss a young man on the first date, and that if he tried to impose a kiss on her at that time, it would be their last date. Talk about a young lady with self-esteem and with a sense of knowing who she is! Somewhere there surely were two very proud parents, as I'm sure they knew her conservative stand.

You might be interested in knowing that studies reveal that young people who think casual kissing is an acceptable social gesture soon become bored with a simple kiss. When the kiss loses its true value, increased physical involvement occurs.

And so, with all forms of physical expression, you are going to have to decide how sacred you want your expressions to be. I suspect that if you are a young man who is concerned about honoring his priesthood or a young lady who is preserving herself for the right time and place and partner, then your expressions will take on a more spiritual perspective.

If not on the first date, just when does a kiss become appropriate? As our previous discussion suggested, there is no pat answer for this question. It must be considered on an individual basis. Not long ago I attended a banquet where a college football coach was speaking. He mentioned that one of his players, who happened to be an all-American, was highly respected by his teammates. The coach said that when this young man began dating his future companion, together they agreed not to kiss until their marriage at the altar in the temple. Feeling that a kiss was this special and sacred, they set this as their goal—then reached that goal.

Certainly this example is unusual and, I suspect, extreme for most of us. Even so, the important point is that they shared the same values and together allowed the kiss to become a very special event in their relationship. Because of this, it will always be a very special symbol of their love for each other.

One young lady came into my office with the concern that the only type of boy she could attract was one who was, in her words, "on the make." I asked her how free *she* was with her affections, and she immediately knew what I was driving at. Although it was embarrassing for her to admit it, her pattern was to make out with everyone she dated.

Whether or not you are aware of it, each of you has a reputation which you either live up to or down to. Your actions on dates will soon establish your reputation with your peers.

It was Ninon de Lenclos who said, "That which is striking and beautiful is not always good; but that which is good is always beautiful." If you hold sacred the kiss, as well as other affections, you will be respected in our Heavenly Father's eyes and be beautiful to yourself and to those who mean the most to you.

Is it right for me to date someone not of our faith? This issue is truly one of the most perplexing problems that parents must deal with. It is also a question which almost all teenagers must resolve.

Here is the issue: It is true that you will marry from among those with whom you associate. It is true that you will become like the person you marry. It is true that you cannot expect to change your spouse after marriage; therefore, you should marry your partner with this expectation. *But,* it is also true that "a candle loses nothing by lighting another candle." That is, when you date someone not of our faith, you could be the missionary who brings that person into the Church.

What, then, are you to do?

It has been my observation that young people who marry out of their own faith immediately have a strike against the solidarity of their relationship. More often than not, this becomes a thorn in their marriage—especially when children come along. Ofttimes this problem becomes so acute as to be one of the wounds which causes the marriage to die. This is particularly so when one or both partners feel strongly about their own religion.

I have also seen many outstanding young people accept the gospel after being introduced to it by someone they knew and cared for on a dating basis. In fact, during one of my years of teaching seminary at East High School in Salt Lake City, a total of fourteen young people (all regular seminary attenders) were brought into the Church. Each of these has now been married in the temple and is enjoying the full blessings of an eternal family unit.

Because of these observations, I have adopted the following philosophy, which I often share with young people who are faced with this dilemma.

If you are just beginning to date, or if you are dating simply for fun and enjoyment as well as for personal development, casually dating someone of another faith can become a "light their candle" experience. If, however, you are in your late teen years or older, use a great deal of discretion. Perhaps the most important thing for you to remember is that your parents love you more than anyone else does. They also know you more thoroughly, and they have been given a stewardship over you. Such love, knowledge, and stewardship gives parents special insight and understanding into your personality, your needs, and your capabilities. You will do well to seek their counsel if this question applies to you.

Let me share one personal experience. With our six dating-age children, we have had only two instances where going on a date with someone of another faith was presented. In one instance our son asked a nonmember on a date. In the other our daughter was asked out by someone of another faith. Because of my relationship with these two children, I was able to sit down with each one (on the two separate occasions) and ask them about their approaching date.

In our conversations, I asked each of them about the standards their dates maintained—their modesty of dress, their grooming, and then their *light*. We talked about the Light of Christ that all individuals are born with, and in both instances my children indicated that these dates were filled with this light. I then took the opportunity to talk about the gift of the Holy Ghost that they, as members of the Church, had been given. I told them that their mother and I expected them to be the leader in their relationship with their dates and to have a prayerful heart as they went on their activities.

I'm pleased to report that in both instances a good time was had by all. Our children truly did have the opportunity to "light their candle." While neither child dated these friends often, the young lady who dated our son showed up at his mission farewell (almost three years after their date). She came to our home afterwards, and she wrote him a special note indicating that she knew he would be a dedicated missionary and that he would be in her prayers.

Now, that was a lengthy treatise of our own family's experience. The important thing is that each child listened to my counsel, as their father, and their testimonies of their own unique identity as a Latter-day Saint increased in the process. My counsel to you therefore, is to lean on your parents, if possible, or on the counsel of your Church leaders. They know you, and they can direct you in the correct path.

For those of you who are older, my advice becomes one of even greater caution. The Brethren have counseled that as we approach the time in our lives when we are selecting our eternal mate, we should date only those of our faith. I recently met with one young lady, age nineteen, who was totally smitten by a young man who was not a Latter-day Saint. They were attending a university in the East, and both wanted to date and to explore the feelings they were having for each other. To make a long story short, this young lady was such a good example that her friend requested missionary discussions and was soon baptized. Following the baptism this couple began dating, and eighteen months later the young man began serving a full-time mission in South America. The girl, although not formally engaged, felt that both were in love with each other and that if their feelings persisted, they would marry following this young man's mission.

The point is this: A Latter-day Saint young lady, having strong feelings about someone of another faith, really *did* light his candle. She informed me that if he hadn't searched and gained a testimony of the Church, she would have simply wished him well and then gone on her way to other relationships. Following the Spirit and the counsel of her parents (who flew from Salt Lake City to the East Coast to attend the young man's baptism), she remained true to herself.

How do you politely say no to someone who has asked you out a number of times but you don't want to accept the date? In counseling with numerous young people who have encountered this situation (just as most of us have, at one time or another), I have said this: Being emotionally honest and mature is the only way to respond. Being emotionally honest is making the decision to tactfully "say it like it is." Being emotionally mature means that you are mature enough to give an honest expression of your feelings without belittling the one asking you out.

Regardless of how socially honest and mature a person is (either a young lady or a young man), there is still the temptation of telling a "white" lie (if there is such a thing). The sad thing is that if the person constantly makes up shallow excuses, the pursuer keeps at it, and the experience repeats itself again and again.

If and when this happens, if you are dating someone else that you like, simply tell the pursuer this. Thank them for asking you, but indicate that you are in another relationship right now and aren't interested in dating anyone else. If you are not dating someone else but still do not want to date this person, just honestly tell them that you would rather be on a friend basis than a dating basis with them.

Believe it or not, people appreciate others who are honest enough to tell them the truth rather than make up one excuse after another, causing this pursuer repeated rejection. So, say it like it is—in a tactful and polite manner—and you will be glad you did.

What do boys and girls look for in each other? In asking this question of students I taught at three different seminaries and at Brigham Young University, I received the following responses, listed in priority from those traits that were mentioned the most to those that were mentioned least. I must add that I told my students that it was a given that physical attraction was the first thing that attracted members of the opposite sex to each other and to not consider good looks at this time.

The boys, both in high school and in college, answered in the following manner:

First and foremost, they liked girls who were real, who weren't phonies or put-ons.

Second, the boys appreciated girls who were feminine and who dressed nicely and wore makeup to enhance their beauty.

Third, these same boys appreciated girls who didn't gossip or malign other girls behind their backs.

The girls, again both in high school and in college, gave the following responses about what they looked for in boys:

First, the young women liked young men who were honest and open rather than guys who appeared to always play games with their words.

Second, they liked young men who were not arrogant but were genuine and humble.

Third, the young ladies looked for young men who showed them respect and who weren't just after their bodies.

I don't know how you would rank these traits or whether you would have others on your list of "what to look for," but I suspect the above personality traits are important to you, as they were to these young people.

Because my parents don't like my boyfriend (or girlfriend), they make it really difficult for me. They don't know him (or her) very well, but because we're getting serious, they say that I am too young, and they won't even try to get to know or accept my partner. Perhaps the parents in question aren't really against the dating partner but simply object to their child's steady dating at this point in life. Or, perhaps the parents see worrisome things in the dating partner or are receiving danger signals for their child and so are expressing concerns of protection for their child.

Let me make a suggestion to you at this time. When you feel that a communication gap is developing between you and your parents, take the initiative to go to them with your feelings. You should give your parents the courtesy of listening to their feelings, and no doubt they will offer the same courtesy to you. When parents find that you are capable of discussing a problem in a mature manner, they begin to have more trust and confidence in you, and they begin treating you more like an adult.

Another thought is this: Professional research has shown that parents really do have a "feel" or a "sense" of how potentially successful their child's relationship might be. This is especially true for parents of young ladies. There is a high correlation between how parents of a young lady feel about their daughter's relationship and the potential success or failure of that relationship. If a parent is experiencing discomfort or concern, be mature enough (and trust your parent enough) to follow his or her guide.

As you consider what I have related above, let me teach you what is called the Emotion Principle. This principle states that the more emotionally involved you are in a relationship, the harder it is to objectively deal with the health of the relationship. Stated more simply, our emotions get in the way of our reasoning power. Therefore, listening to parents and other leaders or friends, if they have doubts, is a very mature and timely thing to do.

It is a real hassle when my parents go through the "board of review" questions: Is he a Mormon? What is he like? Are his parents active in the Church? What kind of

boys does he hang around? Does he attend seminary? How long is his hair? Every time it's the same thing! I wonder if they are ever going to trust me about who I'm going to date! Although it may be difficult for you to believe, there are two different reasons parents ask questions about your dating partners. One or both reasons may exist in your particular case.

It may help you understand if you try and place yourself in your parents' shoes. The first reason is positive, and should make you feel grateful for having parents who sincerely feel this way.

1. Most parents are genuinely concerned. Regardless of whom you are going out with, they want the best for you. The answers to their questions provide a signal to them as to the type of person you are dating.

2. The second reason they ask these questions could be because of your previous dating record. If you have given your parents cause for concern by dating questionable people, they will "hassle" you. I have found that those of you who gain the trust and respect of your parents do not receive constant questioning from them.

How do I get out of a dating relationship that has become stale? One of the problems with steady dating, particularly for young daters, is that of being labeled as going with just one other person. This is especially difficult for a young lady, as in our dating society a young man usually has the prerogative of asking out whom he wants to when he wants to. Still, both boys and girls often choose to exclusively date each other, and so they become an "item." When this takes place, they become more and more involved and bonded to each other, even if they are uncomfortable doing so. At this point their relationship becomes a habit, and they often begin to resent the tied down feeling that they have.

If you are in a relationship that is becoming stale, or that is losing its excitement and energy, simply announce your feelings to your dating partner. Tell your partner that you would like to take a time-out from your relationship right now and that you want to date others. Tell them that if your feelings change and you want to date them again, you will get in touch. Conclude your conversation by thanking them for all the good times you've shared and for the things you've learned from them. Be honest, but tell them what their special qualities are and how they have added to your life.

It's amazing how simple this getting-out process is, yet many young people, young ladies especially, choose to keep "gutting it out" with a dating partner rather than to proactively deal with their own feelings and needs. Remember the proactive versus reactive mode you get in, and then respond proactively! Choose to be dating someone because you want to, not because you have been labeled or because you feel you have to.

In Conclusion, Establish Ideals

As you reflect upon the issues discussed in this chapter, please do yourself the favor of considering them without becoming defensive. A great deal has been said about heeding the counsel and advice of parents and Church leaders. Perhaps you can best understand parents' feelings as you read this poem:

> I must not interfere with my child, I've been told,
> To bend his will to mine, or try to shape him through
> my mold.
> Naturally, as a flower, he must unfold.
> Yet, flowers have the discipline of wind and rain;
> And, though I know it gives the gardener pain,
> I've seen him use his pruning shears to gain
> Strength and beauty for blossoms rare.
> Thus he tends what's in his care
> As the Master-florist tends his lilies fair.
> I do not know, yet it seems to me,
> That only weeds are left to unfold naturally.
>
> —Author unidentified

A young friend, crying uncontrollably, came to visit me. She was in the process of breaking up with her steady boyfriend. She had initiated the breakup because she had finally come to realize that he was like an unpruned weed and that she didn't have the necessary "pruning shears" to assist him as he needed. Not only was he destroying himself, but his persistent sexual advances were beginning to kill her desire to remain virtuous, as she desperately wanted to do. Although this young man was a member of the Church, he no longer attended his meetings or honored his priesthood. Rather, he scoffed at her for the priorities she had established in her life. You see, he had been left by his parents "to unfold naturally," with virtually no restraints.

It is frightening to see how easily we are influenced by the fads of the day. Especially in our media-orchestrated day, every change in fashion makes us want to change our wardrobe or our hairstyle or perhaps even our thinking. We can especially see this every day on television—not just in the powerful and suggestive sitcoms but also in the explicit talk shows that interview young people and their parents on a vast array of issues. The shows themselves have become R- and even X-rated, and they influence the fertile minds of the young people watching them.

An interesting illustration of how you can respond to social pressure is found in the ocean when the ice is breaking up. You can observe the wind, the waves, and the surface ice moving in one direction; yet in the center of the movement you can see an iceberg moving serenely in the opposite direction. The explanation for this phenomenon is that the deeper currents are not influenced by the wind and the surface ice. Since the iceberg extends deep into the ocean, it is able to move quietly on its chosen course.

So it is with you. If you are well rooted in your principles, you will not be influenced by every wind that blows but will continue on your chosen course. Knowing how powerful and pervasive social pressures are on today's youth, I have tremendous admiration for those who chart their own course and who lead out by keeping in tune with the promptings of the Holy Spirit.

5

The Magic of Falling in Love

Paraphrasing from an unidentified writer, I would like to share one of my most favorite quotes: "Infatuation is when you think he's as sexy as Robert Redford, as smart as Henry Kissinger, as noble as Ralph Nader, as funny as Woody Allen, and as athletic as Andre Agassi. Love is when you realize that he's as sexy as Woody Allen, as smart as Andre Agassi, as funny as Ralph Nader, as athletic as Henry Kissinger, and nothing like Robert Redford in any category—but you'll take him anyway!"

Ahh . . . *love!* The most peaceful, exciting, thrilling—and yet troublesome—part of life. There are no other feelings like it, and everyone wants to be in love.

Although there are many different types of love, for our purposes at this time we will concern ourselves only with romantic love. It is this set of emotions, after all, that begins nudging—and ultimately accelerating—a couple to the marriage altar.

There are some who feel that romantic love, as it were, is shallow and temporary. They feel that it is a false love and that a lasting relationship cannot sustain it. From my experience of twenty-seven years of marriage, however, I beg to differ. Rather than thinking of romantic love as a false love, I think of it as a prelude to eternal love. I remember that the last time my wife and I purchased Valentine's Day cards and gifts for each other, there was a flurry of emotions in my heart as I thought of showing her how romantically involved I am with her. Later, as we exchanged gifts and kissed, we enjoyed the same chemistry that caused us to marry in the first place. As my fifteen-year-old son would say, it was sweet!

And so, you may ask, just what *is* romantic love? Perhaps you think of it as being the feelings between a young man and a young woman that become so compelling that these individuals want to marry and to become "one flesh" for the eternities. Or, perhaps you think of it as a fleeting thing that comes and goes with the stages of the moon, causing a person to move in and out of love on a somewhat regular basis.

When two people begin dating, they may first experience the "fluttering heart" feeling. This feeling, if nurtured, quickly blossoms into romantic love. We watched our son and his bride experience this blossoming of romantic feelings as they met, fell in love, became engaged, and then married—all in one semester of college! Both had served full-time missions, however, and each had dated extensively, so they were pretty well primed to recognize the surfacing emotions of true love.

If, as in their case, a relationship is allowed to deepen, the romantic feelings begin to expand and take on additional meaning. When true love develops, a couple does not have to be wrapped up in each other's arms to experience the joys of their relationship. They become excited and involved with helping the partner realize his or her potential. This feeling takes on added meaning for a married couple as they share the birth of each of their children.

A good friend of mine once expressed that love is not a discovery but is truly an art. We do not merely "fall" into real love—only through sharing and giving can we develop the art of loving. Even so, we do pass through the zany phase of being "out of our gourd" for someone. Someone once offered this as a definition of love: "Love is a feeling that you feel when you feel that you're going to feel a feeling that you've never felt before!"

This phase is expressed in a slightly different way with the following lines from a song:

> I climbed up the door, and opened the stairs;
> I said my pajamas, and put on my prayers;
> I turned off the bed, and crawled into the light;
> And all because you kissed me good-night.
>
> —Eddie Pola and George Wyle

On one occasion I was counseling an engaged couple and they were talking about how "crazy in love" they were. They both said they felt as if they were seventeen or eighteen years old. The great part of this story is their true age: the man was seventy-six years old, and the woman was seventy-four! Both of them had lost their spouses in death, and now, after years of being alone, had found a feeling that was refreshing to observe.

Three Types of False Love

While it is hoped that you are considering romantic love as a true and valid set of emotions, and not a false notion, there are false and temporary types of love. Three of these are:

1. Falling in love with love
2. Falling in love with being loved
3. Infatuation

You likely know individuals who are constantly falling in love with love. They are either so desperate for affection or so shallow in their ability to form meaningful relationships that they simply fall in love with anyone. As a seminary teacher, I knew many students who just had to have a boyfriend or girlfriend. These individuals did not actually love the person they were dating (or that they were dreaming of dating); they loved the emotion of love for its own sake. For them, the emotion was usually fleeting, as they were always falling in love with someone (as long as that person wore a dress, or pants—whichever they didn't wear!).

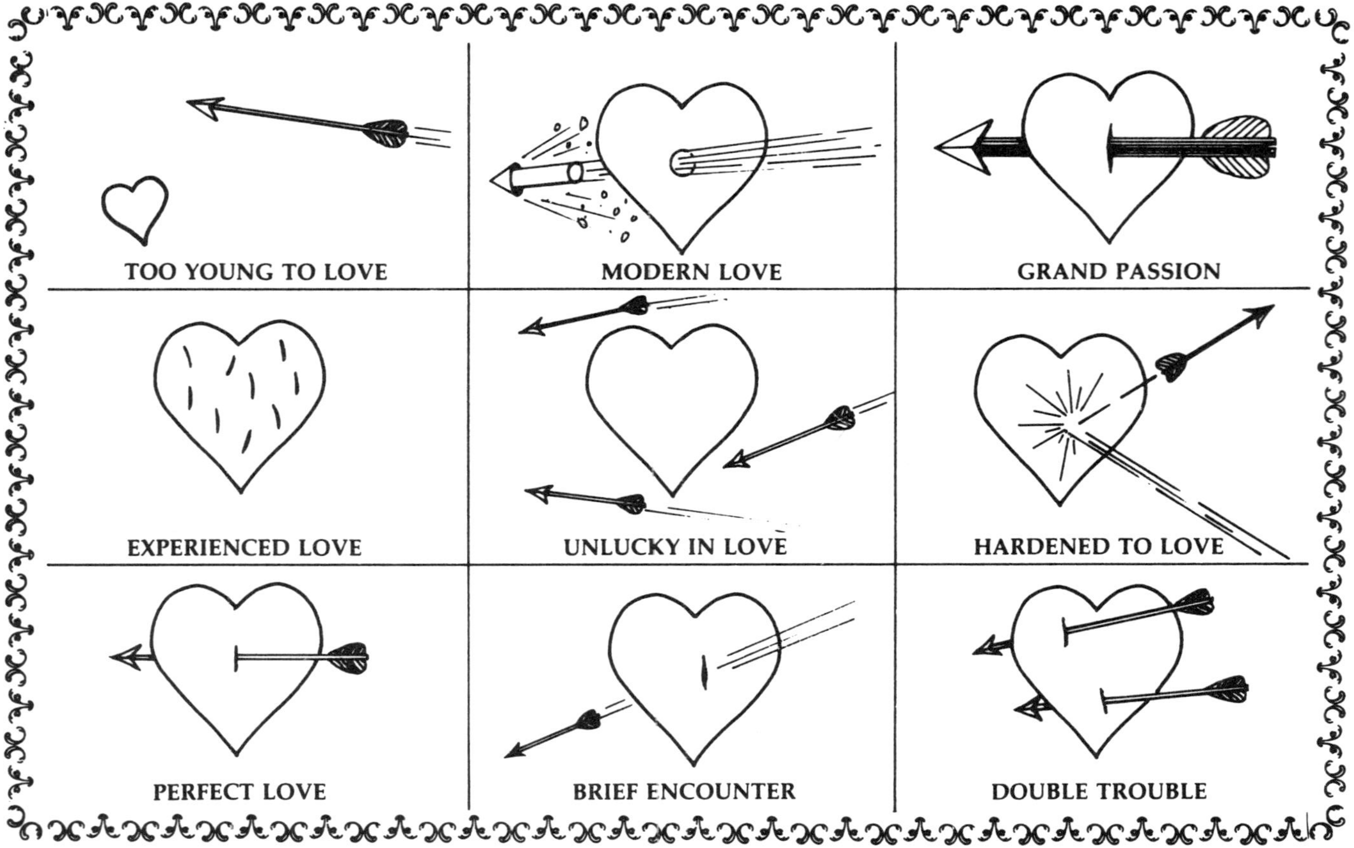
TOO YOUNG TO LOVE
MODERN LOVE
GRAND PASSION
EXPERIENCED LOVE
UNLUCKY IN LOVE
HARDENED TO LOVE
PERFECT LOVE
BRIEF ENCOUNTER
DOUBLE TROUBLE

The second type of false love—falling in love with being loved—is a need-fulfilling emotion. This is apparent with many early teens, as well as with those seasoned daters who are unable to maintain lasting relationships. As I have watched these people express their needs and feelings, I have found that they are often lacking loving relationships within their homes or within their peer relationships. To fill this void, they grasp onto any relationship available—just because they are so needy.

The final type of false love—that of being infatuated—is the one most often mentioned when considering immature and short-term relationships. To help you more fully understand the differences between infatuation and true love, read through the following comparisons. Although it is a lengthy list and will take you a few minutes to work through, I think that making these comparisons will help you—at the right moment in your future—when you are trying to determine just how strong your emotions of love are. Just a thought: As you read through these comparisons, circle the ones that apply (or perhaps did apply) to a given relationship.

Infatuation	*Love*
Tends to be more frequent among young adolescents in early teens	Tends to occur first in late teens and in the twenties
Frequently being involved with more than one boyfriend or girlfriend	Not frequently going with more than one partner
Tends to last but a short time (usually only a few weeks)	Most cases last over a long period of time
Often happens soon after a previous involvement has ended	More slowly develops after a relationship has ended
Is often the name given to past relationships	Often used to refer to present relationship

Infatuation	*Love*
Focuses more frequently on an unsuitable person	Usually refers to a suitable person
Parents often call it this when they disapprove	Parents tend to approve
Focuses on a few traits; mostly physical thrill	Broadly involves the entire personality
Less frequently accompanied by ambition and wide interests	Brings new energy and ambition and more interest in life
Feelings of guilt, insecurity, and frustration are frequent	Associated with feelings of self-confidence, trust, and security
Tends to be self-centered and restricted	Accompanied by kindlier feelings toward others in general
Boredom is frequent when there is no sexual excitement or social amusement	Joy in many common interests and an ongoing sense of being alive when going together—precludes boredom
Little change in relationship with the passing of time	Relationship changes and grows with further association, developing interest and deepening feelings
Problems and barriers are often disregarded; problems are idealized rather than faced with reality	Accompanied by willingness to face reality and to tackle problems realistically
Almost always leaps quickly into bloom	Usually takes root slowly, and it always grows with time

Infatuation	*Love*
Usually accompanied with a sense of uncertainty; you are stimulated and thrilled, but you are not really happy; you are filled with feverish excitement; you are miserable when your partner is absent	You have a calmness about your relationship; you have a deeper excitement that dwells on the meaningful relationship you have rather than on always being in the other's presence
You often lose your appetite. You just don't want food. You can't study. You can't keep your mind on your work. You're most likely short-tempered and rather unpleasant with the family	You have your "emotional" head on your shoulders. You work harder because of life's meaning. You are happy and pleasant to be around
Brings the feeling that you must get married right away. You can't wait—you must not take the chance of losing him or her	Though you may prefer to marry at once, you know that you can wait. You are sure of one another. You plan your future with complete confidence
Actually stems from a desire for self-gratification. The young man or woman is often a "hero" and popular person in your crowd. Or this person may be brilliant and you wish identity with him or her. You want others to know that you have been chosen by this person	There is always deep concern for the welfare of the loved one. Outside criticism does not dull your attachment. It sharpens it. Misfortune which may take away his or her "hero" status is of no consequence to you
Largely a matter of sex. If you are honest, you will	Sex is a natural and spontaneous part of love, but

Infatuation	*Love*
discover that it may be difficult to enjoy each other unless you are leading up to necking	only a part. If your love is real, you will enjoy comradeship with the loved one. You can have fun together without necking. You are friends as well as lovers. You like each other
Infatuated couples find it easy to disagree	When in love, although your personalities may be quite different, there is a willingness to hear the other side, to give as well as to take, to compromise
Frequently brings with it the inability to trust the partner. When away from you, you wonder if your partner is with another girl or boy. You're jealous when your partner laughs with another person or dances with them. You wonder how much you can believe of what your partner has told you	Love understands that your partner may enjoy another dance, another laugh, with no reflection upon the relationship with you. There is a sense that you each belong to each other, that all others are outside
You may "fall" into infatuation	You never "fall" in love, but rather you grow in love
Might possibly lead you to do things of which you would not ordinarily approve—things for which you would be sorry later	Love will cause you to respect and trust your partner, and therefore will not allow you to dishonor your partner or yourself. Love leads you up. It makes you look up. It makes you a better person than you were before

Interact, Enjoy, and Love

Interact is a simple word and initially may not seem to have much to do with love. But you will actually have few rewards in a relationship if you don't interact. When you're able to interact with your partner, just being together makes you happy—it's not so much what you do when you're together, but simply that you spend time together. It's a perfect time to share your past with each other, to talk about what's happening now, and to plan for your future.

Our third son, Jeremy, was engaged to a beautiful young lady named Cheri. Although Jeremy's seminary teacher lined them up right after their sixteenth birthdays, they didn't even hold hands until two months after Jeremy returned from his mission. They dated off and on, as friends, and wrote a few times during Jeremy's mission. What they *did* on their dates, and then in their letters, was interact. They shared so much about themselves, and their love for the Savior and his gospel, that they fell in love with their level of communication and interaction long before they grew to love each other.

President Spencer W. Kimball said "Love is like a flower, and, like the body, it needs constant feeding. . . . Love . . . cannot be expected to last forever unless it is continually fed with portions of love . . . [and] expressions of gratitude." (*Marriage and Divorce* [Salt Lake City: Deseret Book Co., 1976], pp. 22–23.) Expressions of gratitude that provide positive moments of interaction thus become the nourishment needed for love to grow. Be expressive; tell your partner how you are feeling, and in the spirit of honesty say what you are experiencing in your heart. If you want to know what kind of interaction and feedback you will receive from a partner when married, just step back and examine how expressive your dating partner is now.

The Unloving

We have discussed how well a person interacts and expresses feelings of love. Let me now flip the coin over and expose you to what makes a person find it difficult to love. The following observations are based on a discussion of this subject in a book by Kenneth L. Cannon called *Developing a Marriage Relationship.*

The unloving individuals have few or no friends. They find what is wrong with people more quickly than they find what is right with them. They tend to hold themselves aloof and to withdraw. Such a person may make an exception for you and pour all of their love in your direction—if you, yourself, have a great capacity for loving.

Inability to love is also manifest through feelings that "nobody loves me" or "nobody understands me." This person who always feels misunderstood is usually the same person who doesn't understand or try to understand others.

An unloving person is often one who is unable to say no. This person very frequently appears to be loving but feels a compulsion to please everyone—mostly out of fear of rejection.

A final characteristic of the unloving is that of self-absorption. It is true that a person must have a good self-image and hold him or herself in high esteem. A person who is self-absorbed, however, has little concern for others.

How Do I Know If I'm Really in Love?

After reading the materials contained in this chapter, perhaps a few final thoughts could be considered. First of all, real love includes a strong feeling toward a person based on sharing fundamental goals, aims, and standards in life. You will find that attraction grows as you and your partner discover common ground in your life's values.

Real love surfaces when you feel that a person would make an excellent father or mother of your children. You may not have thought of this, but it is very important. I'll never forget the day one of my seminary students came into my office to talk about her boyfriend. They were just concluding their senior year and felt at the time that they were very much in love. Her concern, however, was that this boyfriend yelled, swore, and belittled his little brothers and sisters. She was afraid this would be the way he would treat his children. I told her that unless he did some serious repenting and changing, she was absolutely right. His behavior frightened her to the point that she finally broke up with him—then married one of the kindest men I have ever met. This young woman loved her husband romantically, but she also loved him for his Christlike nature and disposition.

A couple in love develops a "we" feeling. As they come closer together, they do more planning and thinking about the two as a unit and less about themselves as individuals. Genuine love is unselfish and shared. The welfare of the couple is all-important.

When you are truly in love, you think as much of your partner as you do of yourself. You should have high self-esteem, as we discussed earlier; but in a successful relationship you will need to feel just as strongly toward your partner.

When love is real, your partner is a genuine companion to you. This means all the time, not just when you are dressed to the hilt and it's party time. Real sweethearts feel comfortable together and enjoy each other's company in simple, everyday activities.

As a final thought, in order to love someone a romantic attraction must be present. This is not enough by itself, but when it accompanies other favorable characteristics, it adds warmth and zest to a relationship.

Conclusion

You have gained a great deal in reading this chapter if you now realize that love is learned and not simply a set of unexpected emotions. We all pass through stages of learning as we reach for true love. Perhaps you have been infatuated, or have been in love with love, or have even been in love with being loved. You would be unusual if you hadn't experienced at least one of these false loves. You may have even felt unloving at times and wondered if you could ever really love someone enough to fulfill their needs and make them happy. Such relationships and feelings give us a comparison against which we can measure true love.

The development of a lasting love could be compared to climbing a ladder and reaching a higher form of love at the top. It is my hope that you will marry when you are high on that ladder and that you will continue climbing and growing together for the rest of your lives.

6

The Power of Moral Cleanliness

Sex Versus Love

In the previous chapter, we discussed the three false loves, especially focusing on the imitation of infatuation. As you recall, several comparisons dealt with prematurely expressed sexual intimacy. We then contrasted this with how a couple responds (or does not prematurely respond) when they are truly in love.

At this time, I would like to invite you to take a closer look at sexually oriented relationships contrasted with those which are centered around a deep and abiding love. Although you may not presently be in love, there will come a time when you can refer back to this list and gauge what you have, or don't have, in a given relationship:

Sex	*Love*
A biological need	A psychological need
Experienced primarily in the erotic zones of the body	Involvement of the total personality
Objectless—anyone will do	Searches for a specific personality

Sex	*Love*
Found in both man and beast	Found only in humans—but not all humans
Very impersonal and casual	Very personal
The partner can become boring or even hateful after satisfaction is reached	The partner is important whether or not there is satisfaction
One looks for different physical characteristics in a sex partner	One looks for both mental and physical characteristics in a love partner
Selfish, seeks personal satisfaction	Concerned with welfare and happiness of partner. Fears calamity or danger for partner
Partner is idolized—something to worship	Partner is idealized—someone to be admired, to become like
Doesn't share pain or joy when other person experiences them	Shares all emotion experienced by the other person
Possible to possess the other person, to force affections upon them	Impossible to possess the other person or to force other person to love you
Concerned only with parts of body	Concerned with heart, mind—the total person
Variety of partners possible—they are easily replaced	Variety much less possible—partner is difficult to replace
Desire comes and goes—very dependent upon moods	Desire remains constant—not dependent upon moods
Deteriorates with age	Grows with age

If I could sum up one trait that encompasses a relationship dominated by sexual expressions, it would be *selfishness*. If you are in a relationship where your partner applies pressure for you to respond sexually, all in the name of "expressing your love," don't buy it! Individuals with this orientation are very self-absorbed and focused on lust rather than on love. As a therapist, I have found that young people who become sexually active before marriage (and don't repent and put their lives in order) usually build a marriage of selfishness in other areas—and have very little chance of their marriage succeeding.

Thus, you can quite accurately predict what kind of a marriage partner you will have by examining how your dating partner either (a) tries to constantly apply pressure for you to respond sexually or (b) sets up boundaries so that the two of you will be protected from the enticements Satan places in your path. Either your partner will honor the priesthood (his or yours), or they will simply want to go as far as they can in exploiting your standards and your body.

President Spencer W. Kimball often remarked that you can't be in love and in lust at the same time. I believe this with all my heart, for those unmarried couples who begin to experience sexual intimacy likewise watch helplessly as their relationship erodes and then washes out like the sands of the sea—leaving each partner wondering what happened to cause such a disaster.

What Happens When Intimacy Occurs?

Studies have found that a definite pattern of behavior follows couples who experience premarital intimacy. Interestingly, this cycle usually begins with young people who leave the counsel of the Brethren behind and date prior to age sixteen. In essence, these studies have found that:

1. Couples who begin to date early also begin to go steady early.

2. When these early daters begin to go steadily, or steady, their relationship begins to revolve around making out and expressing physical affection.

3. Before long, as the sexual part of the relationship begins to dominate, the couple crosses over the line and begins to pet, then ultimately experiences full intimacy.

4. Once intimacy is experienced before marriage, a loss of trust and respect occurs, and partners begin to live a life of sheer misery.

5. When this takes place, these individuals begin to not only hate themselves as well as their partner but also lose sight of far-reaching goals. No longer do they care about college, going on a mission, or temple marriage. The fog becomes very murky, leaving these individuals in a world of hurt!

The "Roquefort Dressing Theory" of Sexual Intimacy

So, how does this all begin? If you have experienced this debilitating process, or if you have a friend who has, then you have certainly asked this question. I would like to answer by sharing an experience that happened to my wife and me at the time we married.

Like most newlyweds, we were totally broke, only we didn't know it. After all, the year was 1967, and I was making a full $1.10 per hour working at McDonald's in Provo, Utah. My wife was working full-time at a bank, and as we recall, she was making a whopping $1.50 per hour!

Still, we had $30.00 in our pockets when married, and so we were loaded! Actually, if I want to be totally truthful, the $30.00 had been given to us as a wedding gift from my high school sweetheart. She was a very giving person (and I think was so thrilled not to be marrying me that she simply wanted to celebrate by sending us such a generous gift). We were thankful because this meant that we could buy groceries and have a healthy start to our marriage.

After receiving this check in the mail, I cashed it, and then we made our first trip to the grocery store. I wasn't prepared for how quickly this money evaporated, however. We walked out of the store a few moments later having spent $19.67 of the $30.00 on groceries!

We carried three full brown sacks out of the store that day, and moments later, when we began to unpack them onto our small kitchen table, I was surprised to pull out of one of the sacks a bottle of Roquefort dressing. Now, you must know that as a young man growing up in rural Nephi, Utah, I had fancied myself a French dressing man. It had become my favorite, and I couldn't imagine anyone—even my new bride—spending 57 cents on a bottle of Roquefort dressing! I'll never forget challenging her on this unreasonable expenditure, only to have her look up at me with her beautiful brown eyes, bat her lashes, and simply say, "Try it, you'll like it."

Well, my mother hadn't raised a fool, so I couldn't throw away what my wife had purchased. So I did try it, although at first it was quite distasteful to me to eat it. Gradually, however, the dressing didn't taste too bad; and you can imagine who went shopping several weeks later and what *he* purchased for another 57 cents! You guessed it—I was the culprit, as I was actually developing a taste for Roquefort dressing. My wife was pleased, and soon this became a standard for our salads. Now, after over a quarter of a century of buying this kind of dressing, I have definitely become a Roquefort dressing man!

The killer to this story, yet one that I must share with you, is that a couple of years ago I came home from work at the same time my wife was unpacking groceries. One bottle especially caught my eye, and as I picked it up, I was astounded that Margaret would have the audacity to spend $1.89 on Peppercorn Ranch dressing! Still, remembering her earlier ploy, she simply batted her beautiful eyelashes up at me and announced, "Try it, you'll like it." Well, you know how I can't throw something away, and so I have tried it—and have likewise begun to develop a taste for this third type of dressing. You see how citified I am becoming!

The point is this: I had no idea, initially, how delicious Roquefort dressing was—that is, not until I began to enjoy it with my salad. I literally developed an appetite for it that now borders on addiction. I have teasingly told young people that I'm so addicted to Roquefort dressing now that, if it were necessary, I would take it through my veins!

So it is with our sexual appetite. During our younger teen years, prior to the time we begin to date, we have little idea how delicious and enjoyable the dating experience is. Once we begin to date, however, our taste buds for the opposite sex begin to blossom, and soon we develop a full-size appetite for being with a partner and enjoying the physical expressions of love that are unfolding.

I feel this is the main reason the General Authorities counsel young people to not begin dating prior to age sixteen. It is not because you aren't trusted, or because they don't feel you would know how to communicate on a date. Rather, they know that, as with Roquefort dressing, once the dating experience begins, the appetite increases, until finally a couple is propelled right into the temple! The appetite becomes a righteous addiction as couples then begin their own families.

As Elder Boyd K. Packer has indicated, the Lord made the procreative power both *strong* and *constant* (see "*That All May Be Edified*" [Salt Lake City: Bookcraft, 1982], p. 181). He did this knowing that the establishment of families in mortality would require that the emotions to procreate have these ingredients. And the Lord has ordained that this power be used only within the context of marriage. In regard to these matters, the Church's 1990 pamphlet *For the Strength of Youth,* under the heading of "Sexual Purity," states:

> Our Heavenly Father has counseled that sexual intimacy should be reserved for his children within the bonds of marriage. The physical relationship between a husband and a wife can be beautiful and sacred. It is ordained of God for the procreation of children and for the expression of love within a marriage: "Therefore shall a man leave his father and his mother, and shall cleave unto his wife: and they shall be one flesh" (Genesis 2:24).
>
> Because sexual intimacy is so sacred, the Lord requires self-control and purity before marriage as well as full fidelity after marriage. In dating, treat your date with respect, and expect your date to show that same respect to you. Never treat your date as an object to be used for your own lustful desires or ego. Improper physical contact can cause a loss of self-control. Always stay in control of yourself and your physical feelings. (Pp. 14–15.)

The Double Funnel Theory of Commitment and Intimacy

The Double Funnel Theory explains not only what happens as you begin to pair off with someone very special but also how you can maintain a temple worthiness until the moment you and your sweetheart walk into the house of the Lord to be worthily sealed as one. As indicated in the figure on page 86, there are two relationship funnels down which a couple simultaneously move as they near the moment of marriage. These are the commitment funnel and the intimacy funnel.

In considering first the commitment funnel, you can see that as a couple begins to date (illustrated by being at the top of this funnel), there is little or no commitment. They date whomever they choose and enjoy any number of social relationships. Gradually, however, as they move down the commitment funnel, they begin to go steadily, then steady. After some time in this committed relationship, they recognize that they are falling (or growing) in love, and so they become engaged. The period of engagement, as we will discuss in the next chapter, becomes a period of further committing as a couple test their feelings of love and determine whether to follow through with marriage. Assuming their feelings to be real, and constant, they will then reach the very bottom of the commitment funnel—and marry.

You should know that in our society, it is usually the young lady who will push the relationship along, nudging it down the commitment funnel. The young man, on the other hand, usually "holds all the marbles" and controls this funnel—it is he who decides to purchase a ring, to "pop the question," and to marry.

The intimacy funnel, on the other hand, is much more complex. There are actually twenty-four steps leading down the intimacy funnel, beginning with the first step of a boy holding a girl's hand. If the boy is successful at doing this, the girl will respond, and they are at step two. Step three becomes more compelling, as the boy loosens his grip on the girl's hand, then intertwines fingers with her. If she responds, they are now at step four. Step five is the "arm around," and step six is where the girl responds.

Double Funnel Theory of Commitment and Intimacy

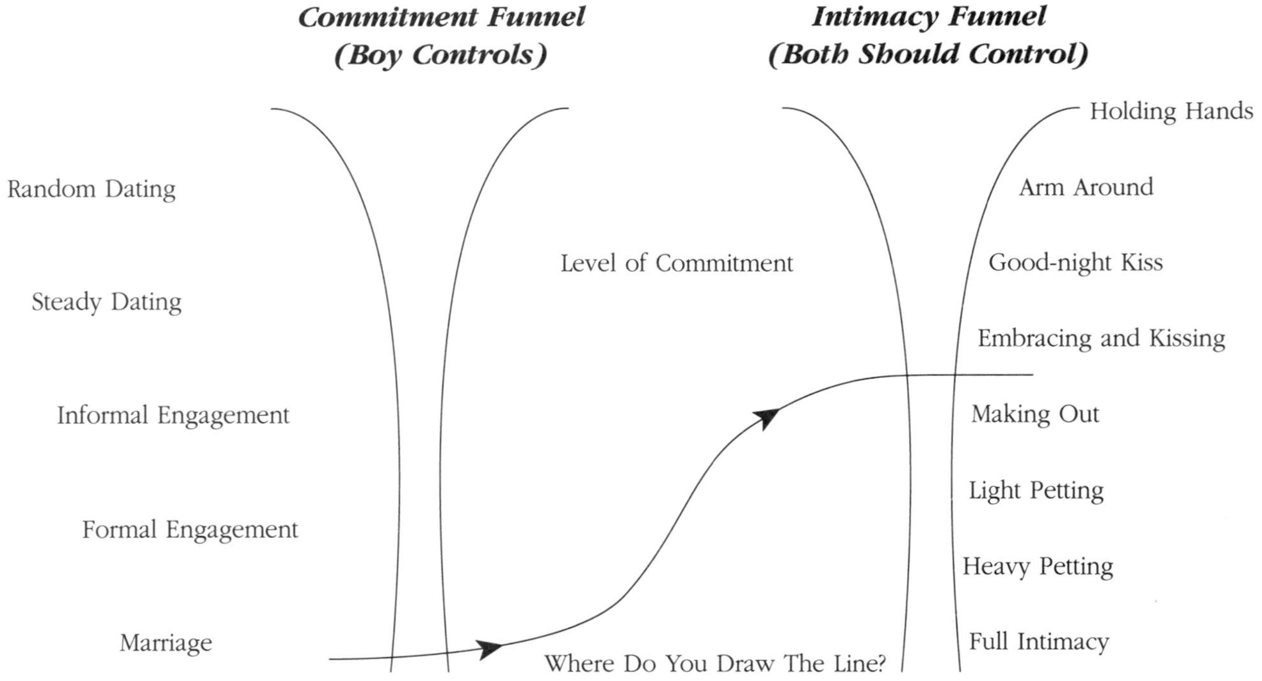

This theory and illustration are adapted from those developed by Carlfred Broderick and Elmer Knowles. Illustration based on that shown in K. L. Cannon's book *Developing a Marriage Relationship*.

Step seven is very magical and takes great courage to pursue—especially in early dating. It is the "good-night kiss," and if it is successful, it is followed by step eight, or the partner's response. Steps nine and ten involve embracing and kissing on a regular basis, as a couple not only enjoys being close physically but is also experiencing a deepening of their feelings of love and the desire to express it.

This part of the intimacy funnel is critical and one that takes a great deal of maturity to monitor. It is also the point in the funnel that separates what is appropriate before marriage and what is not. Steps eleven and twelve, then, involve making out, and this begins to change the "spiritual and physical temperature" in a relationship.

When sharing this theory with young people, I have often asked them what the difference is between "embracing and kissing" and "making out." Once in a great while, someone will be brave enough to announce the correct answer: "Your motive!" This person is right, of course. A couple hugs and kisses in order to *give*—to express feelings of love that are growing inside. On the other hand, couples who begin to have make-out sessions do so in order to *get* turned on. Their motive becomes selfish, as they decide to embark upon a "gland activation" program.

From what I have learned from the General Authorities, and from what professionals who study dating behavior have stated, there is *no* honorable or righteous make-out session prior to marriage. To the contrary, once a couple leaves the safety of "embracing and kissing," their motive changes from one of giving and sharing feelings to one of getting and taking. It is at this moment, I believe, that young people withdraw themselves from the blessings of the Holy Ghost and begin to experience a selfish darkness in their relationship.

Once making out becomes the pattern in a relationship, the funnel becomes so steep that the couple easily falls into the lonely and very painful abyss of petting. Once this barrier is passed, partners are seduced into falling all the way down to an expression of full intimacy, or "going all the way."

I have often told young people that they need to learn to beware of seduction. Seducing someone is taking them where they don't want to go. While many young people think this applies only to petting and full intimacy, it actually begins further up the intimacy funnel. If you do not want to kiss your dating partner but they impose one or more kisses on you, then they have seduced you into going further down this funnel than you cared to go. If a young man has a seduction frame of mind, you can save yourself a lot of grief by simply refusing to go out with him.

Two additional thoughts about the intimacy funnel: (1) While the top part of the intimacy funnel is relatively flat, affording a couple sure footing as they explore their relationship, once the embracing and kissing steps are reached, the funnel becomes very steep and treacherous. (2) Unfortunately, it is usually the young man who tries to push the couple down this funnel. This leaves it to the young woman to be the "enforcer" and stipulate just how far she is willing to go. It shouldn't be this way—especially if the young man honors his priesthood and wants to be worthy of blessing the sacrament and preparing for a mission. Both partners should share the responsibility of monitoring their activity within the funnel and should want to protect their partner from any "accident."

What Happens When a Couple Goes Too Far?

If a couple prematurely date steadily and progress down the intimacy funnel, they will ultimately drop to step twenty-four. Regardless of their intentions, if they center their relationship around making out and getting turned on, they will quickly plummet to the bottom of the funnel. When this occurs, a couple finds themselves in a literal hell. At that point, assuming that they want to repent, they will immediately express sorrow and remorse to each other and then begin to climb out of the intimacy funnel. They go to their bishop, confess their transgression, then begin to back off a little in how often they see each other and what their activities might entail.

Unfortunately, in many cases this tactic works for only about two or three weeks. Then, because the insulation and protection of the Holy Spirit is no longer present in their relationship, they will gradually lose their hold on the side of the funnel and fall harder and more quickly than they did the first time. This time they will be spiritually hammered and will have less of a desire to pick themselves up and make a further attempt to climb out of the dark and lonely plight they are in.

Once a couple loses the spiritual energy to repent, they usually begin to wallow around in the mud of their own making, and a lingering darkness settles in. They no longer see their long-range goals, their relationship with parents and peers begins to deteriorate, and they experience a pain greater than they could ever have imagined. You will know when couples are experiencing this darkness, for they will not only be "draped all over each other" at school but the expression on their faces will be almost lifeless. They will not be able to smile and to be happy but will have almost a glossy-eyed look to their countenances. If you have ever experienced this darkness yourself, then you know what I mean.

From my experience (and I have a file full of letters from young people to prove my point), there is only one way to escape the addicting darkness at the bottom of the intimacy funnel. This solution is painful in and of itself, but it is very necessary. You probably already know what it is—to simply break up.

I tell young people that breaking up with someone in a losing relationship is a lot like cutting off an infected tail of a dog. You don't take the dog out to the woodshed each Saturday morning for sixteen Saturdays (assuming the dog has a sixteen-inch tail) and cut off an inch each time. Such an approach is too painful for the dog. Instead, you take the dog out, stretch its tail out over a log, then take an axe and cut off the tail in one fell swoop. You then quickly get a Band-Aid, cover the bleeding tail stub, and allow a scab to grow over.

So, too, with a relationship that needs to be concluded. You don't cut off one inch at a time by saying things like, "Let's just date once a week or perhaps date someone else in between each of our dates." Such plans simply don't work, no matter how much you feel you love each other. These plans just give you a sense of false hope and betray you by throwing you back down the intimacy funnel just when you think you are making progress.

So, how should you proceed with ending such a losing relationship? As a former bishop, I would recommend the "Eight R's" procedure:

Realize: Be aware that you have made a mistake and have committed a sin.
Regret: Feel deeply sorry inside for what you have done.
Resolve: Make a firm and unwavering decision to change your ways.
Recite: Confess or admit your sins openly to (a) yourself, (b) the person you have sinned against, (c) your bishop, and (d) our Heavenly Father. Your bishop will maintain your trust and will help guide you through the repentance process. He also has the power to grant forgiveness in behalf of the Church and will help you regain your spiritual footing.
Reform: Forsake or discontinue any wrong behavior.
Repay: Make all possible repairs of the damage your sin caused.
Release: Forgive others who have sinned against you. Hold no grudges.
Receive: Accept the gift of forgiveness from others and from our Heavenly Father.

A further thought about breaking up: When you make this decision, it must be final. You will just continue to "bleed" if you continue to call each other, to talk about things, or to interact in any significant manner. Once a few days have passed and the hemorrhaging has finally scabbed over, you will begin to see daylight. You will have met with your bishop, and you will finally begin to feel the atonement of the Savior lifting this transgression from your shoulders.

The Scars of Sin Disappear

Let me shift gears at this point and share an experience I had when I was a young boy attending Primary. One day our teacher stood in front of the class with a piece of paper. She began to describe sins and said that each sin we committed was like adding an additional wrinkle to the paper. She wadded the paper up one wrinkle at a time, then began to smooth the paper back out. She then said that repentance was like smoothing the paper out—but that no matter how hard we smoothed or pressed the paper, we would still never restore it completely, just as we would never be able to completely get rid of the scars of our transgressions.

Years later, as I attended seminary and asked my teacher about this object lesson, he indicated that while my Primary teacher had meant well, she had unknowingly misled us. If repentance is complete—if we truly forsake and then receive forgiveness of something we have done—the Lord truly remembers it no more. This means that if you tragically fall into the bottom part of the intimacy funnel, you can fully restore yourself before the Lord and have him remember it no more. His forgiveness can iron out the wrinkles in the paper to make it completely smooth again.

This is not to imply that such a process is easy or that it can happen with the "wave of a bishop's wand." It is very difficult, especially since Satan will do all within his power to thwart what you are trying to accomplish. You will become discouraged, your self-esteem will be at an all-time low, and you will of course want to be back in the "arms of safety" of your former relationship. Hang on! Lean on your bishop, as well as your parents, for support, and you will ultimately regain the companionship of the Holy Spirit. You will know when this happens, for you will begin to experience a peace "which passeth all understanding."

Consequences of Intimacy Before Marriage

There are many severe consequences which will follow if you allow physical intimacies to take place before you marry. The following points are drawn from an Education Week lecture given by A. Lynn Scoresby.

First of all, early sexual involvement causes you to misinterpret the importance and place sex should have in marriage. Vitally important things such as communication, companionship, problem solving, and decision making are pushed to the background. When physical intimacy occurs, your relationship will begin to center around it, and it will become the dominant force in your relationship.

Another consequence is that your self-esteem—how you feel about yourself—will plummet to depths you can't even imagine. You will begin to hate yourself as well as your partner. There will no more be a foundation of trust and mutual respect, and you will experience depression and sadness like never before. You will feel used and that no one else would want you, so you think you have to continue in your present relationship even if you don't want to.

When self-esteem is lost, you likewise lose sight of long-range personal goals. Think of someone you know who is sexually active, and you will notice that this person has adopted an "I don't care anymore" attitude regarding his or her future. *Now* is all-consuming because of the immediate gratification this person is receiving.

You will also develop a high degree of emotional confusion. You will experience emotions you have never felt before, and you will have no idea how to handle them. One day you might love your partner; the next day that same partner may be hated. One day you may want to change your habits; the next day you simply do not care.

As I mentioned, young people who are sexually active lose the sense of trust that involves being able to predict that their partner will continue to act in a warm, trusting manner. Because there is no commitment, your partner (especially if this partner is a young man) will begin to distance himself from you and to look for "greener pastures." If this loss of trust exists in a relationship before marriage, the chances are great that it will continue through the years of marriage.

Remember this: Love is *not* taking your partner where he or she does not want to go.

Free Love

Free love?
Yes—Isn't that what
  has always made
  love . . . love?
But unrestrained gratification
of one's lusts—
  Isn't it self-control
  that separates man
  from animals?
Yes. Love is free.
  Lust has an
  ugly price.

—Sally Clinton

When your partner imposes himself (or herself) upon you sexually, they do not truly love you but rather "lust" you. When this happens, you become an object with which to satisfy lustful desires, and your relationship will last only as long as you continue to give in to your partner's desires. When you say no and withdraw your affections, your partner will leave you and begin dating someone who also craves lust and sexual intimacy.

Satan's Great Lie: "It's Too Late!"

A good friend of mine, Larry W. Tippetts, wrote the following:

> We are taught that Satan "seeketh that all men might be miserable like unto himself" (2 Nephi 2:27). One of his most successful methods of increasing the number of miserable people in the world is to plant ideas into the minds of those who make mistakes—all of us—such as the following:
>
> "It's too late for me. I've gone too far."
>
> "Who would ever want me after what I've done?"

"What's the use of trying. I can't change the way I am."

"God would never want me in his kingdom."

When you feel those thoughts creeping into your consciousness, just remember that you can't find any of them in the scriptures. You will never hear a prophet, bishop, loving parent, or teacher planting such ideas in your head. That is because those ideas are from Satan, "the father of *lies*." The ultimate danger of this kind of thinking is that we tend eventually to lose all desire to repent and improve. We have the *power* to repent only as long as we have the *will* to repent. . . .

When you find yourself struggling with Satan's lies about repenting, think instead on these truths: God "will with the temptation make a way to escape, that ye may be able to bear it" (1 Corinthians 10:13); and "though your sins be as scarlet, they shall be as white as snow" (Isaiah 1:18). "I do not condemn you; go your ways and sin no more" (D&C 6:35). (*The Choice* [Salt Lake City: Bookcraft, 1984], pp. 34–35.)

How Do I Stay Out of the Intimacy Funnel to Begin With?

This is the part of our discussion that I have been waiting for. If you are a worthy young Latter-day Saint who is honoring your priesthood or the priesthood of those you date, then this is what you may want to do: When you are ready to have one of the most meaningful and crucial prayers of your entire life—perhaps as you conclude your monthly fast next fast Sunday—then retire into your room and close the door.

Once alone, open this book to the page that outlines the Double Funnel Theory. Look at the line that begins at the bottom of the commitment funnel and extends upward and over through the intimacy funnel. This line represents your level of commitment and demonstrates how far down the intimacy funnel you will allow yourself to go prior to your wedding day.

Once you have this line and the funnels in mind, begin your prayer. As you pray, make a promise to Heavenly Father that regardless of any situation that might present itself, you will never pass below your own level of commitment.

Following your prayer, open your journal and record your experience. Outline your promises, and then record your feelings about making such a commitment. One day in the future you may want to read this portion of your journal to your fiancé(e), and you will be glad that you wrote it down.

As you stay true to your commitment to live a virtuous, worthy life consistent with gospel teachings, you will be able to have the Holy Spirit with you, and you won't be led astray in your relationships. Even more, you will be worthy—when the time comes—of guidance from the Lord concerning your marriage decision, thus allowing you to begin marriage with the right person, at the right place, and at the right time.

Could such a prayer and commitment at this time in your life be worth the blessings they could bring in your future? Only you can decide; but, as one who followed this course of action, I can tell you that it has worked and that the price my wife and I paid for our worthiness then really did set us up with a foundation of trust in our marriage.

What's great is that by making this commitment when you aren't in your partner's arms, you are able to place an immediate band of protection around your relationship. Then, whether in three days from now or even three years, you will be able to explain this commitment to the person you are falling in love with, and you can invite your partner to make the same promise. This approach works, as I have learned, and can truly provide safe passage until you ultimately enter into a worthy temple marriage.

Conclusion

In this crucial chapter, we have discussed the following:

1. The differences between a sexual relationship and one of true love.

2. The disastrous consequences of early and steady dating.

3. An appetite theory of sexual motivation—how we, through the dating years, literally develop a God-given appetite for being with a member of the opposite sex.

4. The Double Funnel Theory of Commitment and Intimacy.

5. The divine process of true repentance and forgiveness.

6. An approach for remaining morally clean and preparing yourself for a worthy temple marriage and relationship.

It is my hope that as time passes, and as you season and mature in the dating arena, you will refer back to these pages and give them serious review—certainly not because I wrote them, but because they will give you hope and guidance as you progress through the treacherous waters of being temporarily single.

7

Making the Right Choice

If you are in your early dating years, you are probably wondering why I would include a chapter in this book about choosing the right person to marry. There are several reasons, really. One, which we have already discussed, is that you marry the type of person you date. Another reason is that one day soon, if not *now* for you who are older, you will be making this selection—and you want to get it right the first (and hopefully last) time.

> God help the man who won't marry
> until he finds a perfect woman,
> and God help him still more
> if he finds her.
>
> —Ben Tillett

My wife and I were recently able to spend a weekend in southeastern Arizona, in the stake where Spencer W. Kimball grew up and then served as stake president. While we were viewing the home that he and his wife, Camilla, built, I thought of the unusually unified marriage that must have evolved in that home. I then thought of the advice President Kimball gave on how to select a mate. He said: "Certainly the most careful *planning* and *thinking* and *praying* and *fasting* should be done to be sure that of all decisions, this one is not wrong" (*The Teachings of Spencer W. Kimball,* ed. Edward L. Kimball [Salt Lake City: Bookcraft, 1982], p. 302; italics added).

From what I have read, there are four main stages in selecting a mate. These are:

1. Narrowing the field to a group of eligibles
2. Having an initial attraction to someone
3. Developing a deeper attraction—getting serious
4. Deciding whether or not to marry the person

Stage One: Marrying Within Your Field of Eligibles

From what I have observed, couples in their teens are more apt to not think that they have a choice about whom to marry. Rather, if they become involved in a serious relationship, they allow the convenience of the relationship to naturally push them toward commitment—and toward marriage. Their relationship becomes a habit, and even though there may be many alarm signals going off that indicate the relationship is not right, they feel an obligation to go through with it. They feel this way for one or more of the following reasons:

1. They have gone down the intimacy funnel and so feel stuck in the relationship. They may even be expecting a child and feel that marriage is the only option for them to consider—even if they don't love their partner enough to choose to marry them.

2. They haven't really "shopped around," and so they don't know what (or whom) they might be missing.

3. They don't want to hurt their partner, so they decide to "gut it out."

4. They've told their partner that they will marry him or her, and they don't want to go back on their word.

5. They are secure in the relationship, even though it may leave a lot to be desired.

Believe me when I tell you that choosing a marriage partner for the wrong reasons very seldom leads to a happy and successful marriage. Eternity is a long time to be with someone who isn't right for you. In fact, even one day is a long time to be married to the wrong person. I once considered writing a book called *Equally Yoked or Eternally Choked.* The reason I didn't write it is that we aren't necessarily "eternally choked" if we marry the wrong person. That is simply false doctrine. Each marriage, even if it is sealed in a holy temple, must prove itself. This is done through a lifetime of serving and loving, and evolves very slowly when couples are unsuited for each other.

For now, let's look on the positive side of the coin and consider what it means to marry "within our field of eligibles." We are assuming, of course, that we have several years of dating and relating under our belts and are prepared to select someone who can fulfill our needs and whose needs we can fulfill.

When we look to marry someone within our small group of eligibles, we should look for a person who is as much like us as possible—that is, of the same race, religion, social status, and values. Finding someone who is similar to us eliminates many of the problems that couples encounter in marriage. Susan Marr Spalding said it this way:

> Two shall be born, the whole wide world apart,
> . . . .
> And bend each wandering step to this one end—
> That one day out of darkness they shall meet
> And read life's meaning in each other's eyes.

Stage Two: Initial Attraction

As you know, we are attracted to someone because of a "spark" or "chemistry" that creates a sudden interest. Physical attraction is the first thing that most of us pay attention to when we start going out with someone. We observe whether she is cute, or if he is good-looking. That is usually the first thing our friends ask us if they haven't met the person. It isn't that the person has to be gorgeous or the epitome of masculinity. In fact, most of us are not attracted to people who are a lot better-looking than ourselves.

We are attracted to those who are about as attractive as we are or who are slightly better-looking.

Physical beauty, more than most other things, is in the eye of the beholder. If we are not blessed with a "body beautiful," we are well aware of it by the time we are dating. Most of us have learned that we are all right as we are—freckles, lines, curves (or absence of them), and so on. We are comfortable with ourselves and find comfort in dating people who are like us and who find us as attractive as we find them.

In addition to physical attraction, we are also attracted to people with interests similar to our own. For this reason alone we should develop a wide variety of interests, then place ourselves in social situations where we can meet members of the opposite sex who share these same interests.

Finally, as we interact with the people in our group of eligible partners, we find ourselves ignoring most of them but occasionally being attracted to a few. This is because these few exhibit behaviors that we highly value—spirituality, love of sports, or love of nature, for example. Or we may like their sense of humor or the fact that they have great leadership qualities. They may also be especially kind and tender toward us, or they may behave with an honesty that is totally refreshing. The point is, we learn to value certain behaviors, and this enhances our desire to be with people possessing these behaviors and to explore their potential as marriage partners.

Stage Three: Deeper Attraction . . . or Not!

After the initial chemistry, finding someone with whom we spontaneously "hit it off," we are then influenced by three more factors that may deepen our attraction to this person.

First, we see how similar our values are. That is, do we value religion, wealth, serving others, prestige, cultural events, family? As we begin to date someone, it doesn't take long to learn a lot about their basic values.

Second, we are more deeply attracted to someone when they positively react to the important people in our lives. Likewise, if our family and friends are attracted to the person we are dating, we are then inclined to become more attracted. If they are concerned or worried, however, we too tend to question our relationship with this person.

The final factor that deepens our attraction to a person is how that person responds to us when we reveal ourselves to him or her. If the person you're dating is turned off or uninterested in what you are saying about yourself, then use this as a danger signal. Although you may not have been aware of this factor until now, it really does play an important part in whether you continue to date someone or whether you begin to withdraw.

Stage Four: Marry or Break Up

This last step in the process of selecting a mate usually occurs after we have been going together for a while. We've had the opportunity to observe our partner's core values and personality, and we have learned that we are basically compatible. Our family and friends have begun treating us like an "item" or a pair, and we have very positive love feelings for each other.

Many young couples go through this stage before they get engaged. They talk, think, and pray about whether they ought to marry each other. If they decide to marry, they become engaged. Others go through this stage after the engagement. They decide to get engaged but aren't really sure if they want to go through with marrying this person.

Being Engaged

There are three primary reasons our society has adopted a period of engagement prior to a couple's getting married. First, of course, you get engaged so that you can begin to interact with each other on a much deeper level than before you were engaged. I tell young people that becoming engaged suddenly changes everything. It is like you have been swimming along in the three-feet-deep part of a swimming pool; then suddenly you become engaged and dive way down to the eleven-feet-deep level. It really is a revealing experience, and usually a very fulfilling one.

The second purpose of the engagement is to prepare and plan for your wedding. Although the girl has much more to consider than the boy—the wedding dress, the reception, the announcements, and so on—the boy should be supportive and help with the plans.

The final and most important reason for being engaged is to test your relationship. While in shallow waters, it's pretty hard to gauge how well you swim together. Thus, while diving down and exploring new depths, you find out how compatible you are—as well as how fulfilled you are while experiencing this level of commitment.

One of the real tragedies in our society is the number of couples who marry with one or both partners not feeling good about it. They feel obligated, or they don't want to hurt their partner, or they have a certain level of love—even though they feel hesitant. I tell young people that the time to marry is when both can run to the temple! If either you or your partner is hesitant, for heaven's sake (and for *your* sake), put off your date until your feelings are sorted out.

What If There Are Doubts?

This is a good question, as, at one time or another during their engagement, couples often experience doubts about marrying. The important thing to consider is the basis for the doubts you may be having. That is, if you have situational doubts—you don't think you have enough money, or you don't feel you are personally prepared enough—these doubts are likely not valid. However, if you have personal or relationship doubts—you are unsure of your partner or of your relationship—these doubts need to be dealt with. Let time pass, be prayerful, be worthy of promptings from the Holy Spirit, and interact! If these doubts persist, then you are likely being directed not to marry that person.

Above all, be true to your feelings. Even if it is the night before your wedding, if your feelings are not consistent or totally comfortable, don't go to the temple! I have a younger sister who, in spite of trying to manufacture love feelings deep enough to marry a certain young man, finally announced that she couldn't marry him. Her announcement came after his family drove up from California for the wedding and after all announcements had been sent out. In fact, it was made the night before the wedding!

Well, my sister spent her supposed wedding day returning gifts that had been given, while our parents sat on the steps of the chapel where the reception had been scheduled. They turned friends away all evening; and although it was a very painful experience for them, they were relieved beyond words that my sister had been true to her feelings. She went on to marry a man with whom she is "equally yoked," and she is eternally grateful for having responded to her doubts.

Where's My Man?

At sweet sixteen, I first began
    To ask the good Lord for a man;
At seventeen, as I recall,
    I wanted someone strong and tall.
The Christmas I reached eighteen
    I fancied someone blond and lean.
And then at nineteen, I was sure
    I'd fall for someone more mature.
At twenty, I thought I'd find
    Romance with someone with a mind.
I retrogressed at twenty-one
    And found college boys most fun.
My viewpoint changed at twenty-two,
    When "one man only" was my cue.
I broke my heart at twenty-three
    And asked for someone kind to me,
Then begged at blasé twenty-four
    For anyone who wouldn't bore;
Now, Lord, that I am twenty-five
    Just send me someone who's alive!

—Author unidentified

Your Date with Eternity

The house of the Lord, or the holy temple, is the most sacred place on earth. Beginning with the tabernacle that Moses built in the wilderness (about 1500 B.C.), temples have been available at various times to God's children. Solomon built the first permanent temple from 1012 to 1005 B.C. Over 180,000 workers were employed in constructing this temple, with 3,600 of these being supervisors. It was built in Jerusalem but was later destroyed by the Babylonians. Another temple was built several years afterward, and it was eventually torn down by King Herod in order to construct a new one. The temple built by Herod was the one that existed during Christ's earthly mission. It was destroyed, however, in A.D. 70 by the Romans during a siege that also resulted in the deaths of many Jews.

At this writing, we have nearly fifty temples throughout the world, making the opportunity for marrying in God's house more feasible than ever before. For each of you, a marriage for eternity should be your uncompromising goal. I jokingly tell young people that marrying outside the temple is like kissing your sister—it's a pleasant experience, but not one to remember or to record in your journal!

The first thing you need to do to prepare to attend the temple is to live the basic teachings of the gospel. Those of you who become endowed and then serve missions prior to your marriage will undoubtedly have a head start in terms of understanding the profound nature of temple worship. For now, however, each of you should promise yourselves, your dating partners, and the Lord that you will be temple worthy every day of your life.

If you meet with your bishop to obtain a recommend to perform baptisms for the dead, the questions he asks will determine your worthiness to enter the Lord's holy structure. One of the misconceptions young people have about the temple is that they think they must reach perfection in order to enter and to marry there. In truth, our temple recommends are given to us when we reach a certain minimum level of righteousness. That isn't to say that the minimum isn't high, for it is—but we go to the temple to weed out inconsistencies in our lives and to perfect ourselves "line upon line." The temple is the Lord's university, and we learn about him and his eternal truths there more than any other place.

Not long ago I was visiting with two young people—each eighteen years of age. The young man was preparing for his mission and was planning on sending in his papers in the next few months. We were talking about the great blessings of the temple and how Satan and his host of spirits are not allowed to enter those hallowed walls. I then pointed out to them that one of the great blessings of temple worship is that when we worthily go to the temple we can be free from Satan's nudgings and receive answers to our prayers.

I then shared an experience my wife, Margaret, and I had on October 17, 1967, in the Salt Lake Temple. She had just returned from serving a full-time mission to England, and I had been home from my mission to Florida for about eighteen months. This was a triple date, with her parents and mine being invited along. Although Margaret didn't know what was happening, our four parents did: in my shirt pocket I carried a beautiful diamond ring.

Following our temple session, I asked one of the temple workers if Margaret and I could have prayer in one of the smaller rooms there. Permission was granted, and we left our parents visiting with each other. We entered the room, knelt down, and offered prayer. I was the voice, and as we held hands, I asked Heavenly Father if our feelings were right and if we should marry. Halfway through the prayer, I paused, we opened our eyes, and I took the ring from my pocket and placed it on her left hand. We then finished praying, arose, and briefly kissed.

As we left that small room, we joined our parents and announced to them our engagement. They were happy for us, and even more important, Margaret and I both knew that we had received a confirmation from the Lord that we were, in fact, to spend eternity with each other. The important thing, for each of us, was that we had fasted that day and had entered the temple in worthiness. We had both honored the covenants we had made, and now, at this pivotal moment in our lives—when we needed to make the most crucial decision of our mortality—we had the right to ask and then receive.

After we left the temple we took our parents to Snelgroves for ice cream (although I'm sure that one of them paid the bill) and then we returned to our homes in Provo. It was the perfect date, yet it was overshadowed by our wedding day, two months later, as we worthily married in the historic Manti Temple. We were sealed in the same room that our parents, grandparents, and great-grandparents had married in—and of course this was the perfect beginning to our life together.

In conclusion, let me again go back to that October of 1967. This time, however, let me take you to Salt Lake's Temple Square two weeks before the evening of our engagement. This time we were alone together, attending the Saturday morning session of general conference. Following this session, we walked around the beautiful, flower-laden grounds, then found a small bench to sit on.

As we sat down, I pulled a piece of paper from my inside coat pocket, then read it to my sweetheart, Margaret. It was a poem, actually, that I had written during the last month of my mission. I had left Florida and, with my companion, had reopened the island of Puerto Rico to missionary work. I'll never forget sitting at our small kitchen table in San Juan and banging out the words to this poem on my small black portable typewriter.

Now, here I was, seventeen and a half months later, handing it to the girl of my dreams. At Margaret's suggestion, let me now share it with you:

April 28, 1966
San Juan, Puerto Rico

Dear Dream Girl:

There will be a time in an appointed place for an eternal reason that you and I will once again meet, to fulfill the measure of our creation. To this end I am now preparing.

I say that we will meet again, because as you know, our hearts were one as we progressed in our premortal existence—and then in parting to take our mortal forms on this goodly habitation, we were promised that, in accordance with our righteous deeds and desires, we would be granted the most sacred opportunity and responsibility known to mankind: that of perpetuating our seed in rearing a number of our spiritual brothers and sisters as they leave the presence of our Creator.

Now, Dream Girl, you are no doubt in wonderment as to why my thoughts and heart are turned to you, while I labor as a missionary on this faraway fertile island. You see, Dear One, it has been impressed so firmly on my mind that along with bringing joy to others, we missionaries should evaluate our lives so as to prepare for life with choice spirits such as you, thus making available the opportunity of eternal partnership with God, as we enter into his rest.

I have often felt that although my missionary activity has given my heart more complete joy and satisfaction than any other previous experience in my life, there is still a corner of my heart which is left unexposed to life, left empty to be one day filled and consumed by a God-given gift—your love and sincere devotion.

Is it then with any wonder, my love, that I address you at this time?

Perhaps you may ask, "How is it he knows it is me he at one time revered?" To this let me state:

How is it a bird knows when to turn south, as the leaves turn to brown and to gold?

How is it a lamb, being lost in a storm, can safely return to its fold?

Or what turns in the heart of a man aged with sin, as he kneels now in meekness toward heaven?

I'm sure it's the still, selfsame power from on high. From our Maker it's surely been given.

The prophet has said that I'll know who to marry, by the whispering of that still small voice.

When I find a companion in whose presence I'm inspired, to grow and progress at my choice.

During the past several months, I have encountered mistakes made in homes where the gospel's not been.

And I'm grateful, Dream Girl, that it has charted my course—Yes, I've grown from the things I have seen.

It is true there'll be times when problems we'll face, and Satan will seek to destroy.

Yet, with the priesthood of God protecting our home—Be assured it's true power we'll employ.

Now, Dream Girl, continue pursuing the course; the road that for us is appointed.

Until we kneel in the temple of God, and are made "one" by the Lord's true anointed.

This is my humble prayer and desire.

Preparing to be yours,
B.G.Y.

Now, in hindsight, I understand that I can't be certain whether my future wife and I knew each other in our pre-earth life and that I may have been overstating that part of my letter to my dream girl. The important thing is that both Margaret and I had prepared for this moment and were worthy to receive direction from the Lord regarding our future. This fact has sustained us again and again as we have experienced the passions and perils of family life.

Let me now get back to you.

Each of you are at this very moment writing your own pre-marriage history. Whether you are sixteen years of age and just beginning to date, or twenty-three and right now getting engaged, the issues presented in this chapter, and this book, are compelling to know. As one who was greatly blessed in finding someone suitable to my needs and personality, I likewise wish *you* every success as you date and fall in love. I also wish you great joy as you meet one who fulfills your dreams and with whom you can share the marvelous journey into your eternities.

About the Author

Best-selling author Brenton G. Yorgason is a frequent speaker to youth groups throughout the Church. He is a native of Utah and served a mission to Florida and Puerto Rico, and was set apart as a special missionary while stationed in Vietnam with the U.S. Army. He received a Ph.D. in family studies, with a doctoral minor in marriage and family therapy, from Brigham Young University. He has lectured extensively in the area of marriage and family, and has authored or coauthored several books about premarital and marriage relationships, including *From Two to One, From This Day Forth, Creating a Celestial Marriage, Marriage and Family Stewardships,* and *Sacred Intimacy.*

He and his wife, Margaret, are the parents of nine children. Their son Aaron created the illustrations for this book. The family resides in Sandy, Utah.